Building Impressive Presentations with impress.js

Design stunning presentations with dynamic visuals and 3D transitions that will captivate your colleagues

Rakhitha Nimesh Ratnayake

PUBLISHING

BIRMINGHAM - MUMBAI

Building Impressive Presentations with impress.js

First published: March 2013

Production Reference: 1190313

Published by Packt Publishing Ltd.
Livery Place
35 Livery Street
Birmingham B3 2PB, UK.

ISBN 978-1-84969-648-7

www.packtpub.com

Cover Image by Duraid Fatouhi (duraidfatouhi@yahoo.com)

Credits

Author
Rakhitha Nimesh Ratnayake

Reviewers
Chetankumar Akarte

Christian Ziebarth

Acquisition Editor
Martin Bell

Commissioning Editor
Maria D'souza

Technical Editor
Nitee Shetty

Project Coordinator
Esha Thakker

Proofreader
Maria Gould

Indexer
Tejal Soni

Graphics
Aditi Gajjar

Production Coordinator
Pooja Chiplunkar

Cover Work
Pooja Chiplunkar

About the Author

Rakhitha Nimesh Ratnayake is a software engineer working in a leading software development firm in Sri Lanka. His work there includes planning and implementing projects in a wide range of technologies based on PHP frameworks.

He is the creator of www.innovativephp.com, where he writes tutorials on the latest web development and design technologies. He is also a regular contributor to a number of popular websites such as 1stwebdesigner, the tuts+ network, and the Sitepoint network.

He likes to watch cricket and stay with the family when he isn't working on coding or writing. Make sure to visit him online at www.innovativephp.com and follow him on Twitter at twitter.com/innovativephp.

I would like to thank my parents and my brother for providing great support throughout the book. This was my first book and I really appreciate the encouragement they gave in tough periods while writing the book. Special thanks to Bartek Szopka, who is the creator of impress.js, for helping me in the early stages of this book.

I would also like to thank Packt team members, Shrutika Kalbag for finding my article on 1stwebdesigner and providing me with the idea about this book, Maria D'souza for the support throughout the book and being the editor, and Esha Thakker for being the project coordinator of the book.

Finally, I would like to thank you for reading my book and being one of the most important people who helped me to make this book a success. Thank you.

About the Reviewers

Chetankumar Akarte is an Electronics Engineer from Nagpur University located in central India. He has more than 6 years of experience in the design, development, and deployment of Web, Windows, and mobile-based applications with expertise in PHP, .NET, JavaScript, Java, Android, and more.

He likes to contribute on the newsgroups and forums. He has written articles for Electronics For You, DeveloperIQ, and Flash & Flex Developer's Magazine. In his spare time, he likes to maintain his technical blog http://www.tipsntracks.com to get in touch with the developers community. He has been the technical reviewer for three books published by Packt Publishing. He has released some Marathi and Hindi e-book applications in the Android market (https://play.google.com/store/apps/developer?id=Sahitya+Chintan).

He lives in the hilly Kharghar area of Navi Mumbai with his son Kaivalya and wife Shraddha. You can visit his websites http://www.SahityaChintan.com and http://www.tipsntracks.com, or get in touch with him at chetan.akarte@gmail.com.

I would like to thank my wife Shraddha and my parents for their consistent support and encouragement and my lovely son Kaivalya who allowed me to use his playtime with me to dedicate towards this book. I would also like to thank Packt Publishing for giving me the opportunity to do something useful and especially the Project Coordinator, Esha Thakker, for all the valuable support.

Christian Ziebarth began working on the Web in 1996 when he was informed of GeoCities. He began learning HTML in 1998, CSS in 1999, and was doing things in CSS in Netscape 4 of which only a few people knew could be done at the time. Since 2000 he has worked on many professional web projects of varying sizes and continues to explore new frontiers on the Web. He lives in California and has also lived in Ireland and Hawaii.

www.PacktPub.com

Support files, eBooks, discount offers and more

You might want to visit www.PacktPub.com for support files and downloads related to your book.

Did you know that Packt offers eBook versions of every book published, with PDF and ePub files available? You can upgrade to the eBook version at www.PacktPub.com and as a print book customer, you are entitled to a discount on the eBook copy. Get in touch with us at service@packtpub.com for more details.

At www.PacktPub.com, you can also read a collection of free technical articles, sign up for a range of free newsletters and receive exclusive discounts and offers on Packt books and eBooks.

http://PacktLib.PacktPub.com

Do you need instant solutions to your IT questions? PacktLib is Packt's online digital book library. Here, you can access, read and search across Packt's entire library of books.

Why Subscribe?

- Fully searchable across every book published by Packt
- Copy and paste, print and bookmark content
- On demand and accessible via web browser

Free Access for Packt account holders

If you have an account with Packt at www.PacktPub.com, you can use this to access PacktLib today and view nine entirely free books. Simply use your login credentials for immediate access.

Table of Contents

Preface

Creating presentations and impressing the audience is an important task for people who work as software professionals, marketers, public speakers, or anyone who is familiar with computer-related work. Online presentation creation applications are gaining much more popularity over conventional desktop-based software applications in the recent years. impress.js is a powerful library that eases the task of creating presentations with smooth animations without depending on a software tool. You are no longer limited to desktop tools as these presentations run on any supported browser anywhere on the Internet.

This book consists of several practical real-world examples which go beyond the conventional slide-based presentations covering each aspect of the impress library. A wide range of applications such as content sliders, image galleries, awesome presentations, and complete websites are created throughout the book explaining the techniques in a way that even a beginner can understand.

Understanding how different features work is something we need to know as developers or designers in order to tweak the core library and create our own customizations. Important sections of the impress.js core code are explained in detail with practical examples to make it easier for you to implement new features and enhance impress.js.

By the time you are done with this book, you'll be able to create a wide range of components for websites using impress.js as well as stunning visualizations to impress your audience.

What this book covers

Chapter 1, Getting Started with Impressive Presentations, provides an introduction to presentations with impress.js and its importance. We also create a basic impress presentation with detailed code explanations.

Chapter 2, *Exploring Impress Visualization Effects*, discusses the in-depth usage of impress effects such as positioning, scaling, and rotating using practical real-world examples. impress.js core code is also discussed in detail to understand the implementation of CSS effects.

Chapter 3, *Diving into the Core of impress.js*, is focused on discussing impress.js configurations and the core code required for simplifying customizations to existing features. Usage of impress API, step events, and keyboard configurations is explained using advanced presentations.

Chapter 4, *Presenting on Different Viewports*, explores the use of impress presentation fullscreen, inside a container and mobile devices. Fully functional content slider is created to explain the wide range of uses for impress presentations. Mobile device support and the handling of presentations on different devices is explained in detail throughout this chapter.

Chapter 5, *Creating Personal Websites*, acts as a complete guide to creating personal websites using impress.js. A single page website is developed with commonly-used techniques in web design.

Chapter 6, *Troubleshooting*, covers the compatibility of impress presentations and the necessary information to fix bugs and get support for issues in impress.js. Limitations and possible future enhancements are explained to motivate you to implement your own features for impress.js.

Appendix, *Impress Tools and Resources*, guides you through the available impress.js presentation automation tools and some awesome presentations available online.

What you need for this book

This book assumes that the readers are familiar with the basics of HTML, CSS, and JavaScript. Also, you will need the following things in order to work with this book:

- An Internet connection (to load external libraries and fonts in the demo files)
- Code editor
- impress.js compatible browser

Who this book is for

This book is for anyone who is interested in impressing their audience with stunning online presentations without depending on software applications. The main focus will be for the web designers and developers who are familiar with technical stuff. impress.js is a powerful presentation creation library using CSS transforms, so readers are expected to have the basic HTML, CSS, and JavaScript knowledge for creating impressive presentations.

Conventions

In this book, you will find a number of styles of text that distinguish between different kinds of information. Here are some examples of these styles, and an explanation of their meaning.

Code words in text, database table names, folder names, filenames, file extensions, pathnames, dummy URLs, user input, and Twitter handles are shown as follows: "We can use the `data-rotate-x` attribute to rotate elements around the x axis."

A block of code is set as follows:

```
$(document).ready(function(){
        document.addEventListener
        ("impress:stepenter", function (event) {
            // Code for step enter
        }, false);

        document.addEventListener
        ("impress:stepleave", function (event) {
            // Code for step leave
        }, false);
});
```

When we wish to draw your attention to a particular part of a code block, the relevant lines or items are set in bold:

```
$(document).ready(function(){
        document.addEventListener
        ("impress:stepenter", function (event) {
            // Code for step enter
        }, false);

        document.addEventListener
        ("impress:stepleave", function (event) {
            // Code for step leave
        }, false);
});
```

New terms and important words are shown in bold. Words that you see on the screen, in menus or dialog boxes for example, appear in the text like this: "We can go to the overview of the presentation using the **Overview** button".

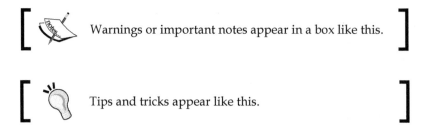

Warnings or important notes appear in a box like this.

Tips and tricks appear like this.

Reader feedback

Feedback from our readers is always welcome. Let us know what you think about this book—what you liked or may have disliked. Reader feedback is important for us to develop titles that you really get the most out of.

To send us general feedback, simply send an e-mail to feedback@packtpub.com, and mention the book title via the subject of your message.

If there is a topic that you have expertise in and you are interested in either writing or contributing to a book, see our author guide on www.packtpub.com/authors.

Customer support

Now that you are the proud owner of a Packt book, we have a number of things to help you to get the most from your purchase.

Downloading the example code

You can download the example code files for all Packt books you have purchased from your account at http://www.packtpub.com. If you purchased this book elsewhere, you can visit http://www.packtpub.com/support and register to have the files e-mailed directly to you.

Errata

Although we have taken every care to ensure the accuracy of our content, mistakes do happen. If you find a mistake in one of our books—maybe a mistake in the text or the code—we would be grateful if you would report this to us. By doing so, you can save other readers from frustration and help us improve subsequent versions of this book. If you find any errata, please report them by visiting http://www.packtpub. com/submit-errata, selecting your book, clicking on the **errata submission form** link, and entering the details of your errata. Once your errata are verified, your submission will be accepted and the errata will be uploaded on our website, or added to any list of existing errata, under the Errata section of that title. Any existing errata can be viewed by selecting your title from http://www.packtpub.com/ support.

Piracy

Piracy of copyright material on the Internet is an ongoing problem across all media. At Packt, we take the protection of our copyright and licenses very seriously. If you come across any illegal copies of our works, in any form, on the Internet, please provide us with the location address or website name immediately so that we can pursue a remedy.

Please contact us at copyright@packtpub.com with a link to the suspected pirated material.

We appreciate your help in protecting our authors, and our ability to bring you valuable content.

Questions

You can contact us at questions@packtpub.com if you are having a problem with any aspect of the book, and we will do our best to address it.

1
Getting Started with Impressive Presentations

Presentations are one of the most effective ways of communicating our ideas to people who are interested in the topic. A perfect presentation will grab the attention of the audience and keep them interested in our ideas, while a bad presentation can bore our audience and ruin our reputation. This means that, the presentation creation tools play a vital role in designing a good presentation.

We used to create presentations with popular desktop programs such as Microsoft PowerPoint and Open Office Impress. Things have changed dramatically now and web-based presentations are gaining more interest from users. **impress.js** is one of the stand out frameworks among the web-based presentation creation libraries and tools. We are going to work on creating impressive visualizations with this framework from here on.

In this chapter, we are going to cover the following topics:

- What is impress.js?
- Built-in features
- Beyond presentations with impress.js
- Why is it important?
- Downloading and configuring impress.js
- Creating your first presentation

Ideally you should have basic knowledge of CSS and HTML to understand this chapter. Everything will be explained using detailed and simple examples and by the end of this chapter you will have the knowledge to create basic presentation with impress.js.

So let's get started!

What is impress.js?

impress.js is a presentation framework build upon the powerful CSS3 transformations and transitions on modern web browsers. Bartek Szopka is the creator of this amazing framework. According to the creator, the idea came to him while he was playing with CSS transformations. `Prezi.com` was the source that got him inspired. On `w3.org` we have the following mentioned about CSS transforms:

> *CSS transforms allows elements styled with CSS to be transformed in two-dimensional or three-dimensional space*

For more information on CSS transformations for those who are interested, visit `http://www.w3.org/TR/css3-transforms/`.

Creating presentations with impress.js is not a difficult task once you get used to the basics of the framework. Slides in impress.js presentations are called steps and they go beyond the conventional presentation style. We can have multiple steps visible at the same time with different dimensions and effects. impress.js step designs are built upon HTML. This means we can create unlimited effects and the only limitation is your imagination.

Built-in features

impress.js comes with advanced support for most CSS transformations. We can combine these features to provide more advanced visualizations in modern browsers. These features are as follows:

- **Positioning**: Elements can be placed in certain areas of the browser window enabling us to move between slides.
- **Scaling**: Elements can be scaled up or scaled down to show an overview or a detailed view of elements.
- **Rotating**: Elements can be rotated across any given axis.
- **Working on 3D space**: Presentations are not limited to 2D space. All the previously mentioned effects can be applied to 3D space with the z axis.

Beyond presentations with impress.js

This framework was created to build online presentations with awesome effects with the power of CSS and JavaScript. Bartek, who is the creator of this framework, mentions that it has been used for various different purposes expanding the original intention. Here are some of the most common usages of the impress.js framework:

- Creating presentations
- Portfolios
- Sliders
- Single page websites

List of demos containing various types of impress.js presentations can be found at `https://github.com/bartaz/impress.js/wiki/Examples-and-demos`.

Why is it important?

You must be wondering why we need to care about such a framework when we have quality presentation programs such as PowerPoint. The most important thing we need to look at is the license for impress.js. Since it is licensed under MIT and GPL we can even change the source codes to customize the framework according to our needs. Also most of the modern browsers support CSS transformations, allowing you to use impress.js, eliminating the platform dependency of presentation programs.

Both desktop-based presentations and online presentations are equally good at presenting information to the audience, but online presentations with impress.js provide a slight advantage over desktop-based presentations in terms of usability. The following are some of the drawbacks of desktop program generated presentations, compared to impress.js presentations:

- Desktop presentations require a presentation creation software or presentation viewer. Therefore, it's difficult to get the same output in different operating systems.
- Desktop presentations use standard slide-based techniques with a common template, while impress.js presentation slides can be designed in a wide range of ways.
- Modifications are difficult in desktop-based presentations since it requires presentation creation software. impress.js presentations can be changed instantly by modifying the HTML content with a simple text editor.

Creating presentations is not just about filling our slides with a lot of information and animations. It is a creative process that needs to be planned carefully. Best practices will tell us that we should keep the slides as simple as possible with very limited information and, letting presenter do the detailed explanations.

Let's see how we can use impress.js to work with some well-known presentation design guidelines.

Presentation outline

The audience does not have any idea about the things you are going to present prior to the start of the presentation. If your presentation is not up to standard, the audience will wonder how many boring slides are to come and what the contents are going to be. Hence, it's better to provide a preliminary slide with the outline of your presentation.

[A limited number of slides and their proper placement will allow us to create a perfect outline of the presentation.]

Steps in impress.js presentations are placed in 3D space and each slide is positioned relatively. Generally, we will not have an idea about how slides are placed when the presentation is on screen. You can zoom in on the steps by using the scaling feature of impress.js. In this way, we can create additional steps containing the overview of the presentation by using scaling features.

Using bullet points

People prefer to read the most important points articles rather than huge chunks of text. It's wise to put these brief points on the slides and let the details come through your presenting skills. Since impress.js slides are created with HTML, you can easily use bullet points and various types of designs for them using CSS. You can also create each point as a separate step allowing you to use different styles for each point.

Animations

We cannot keep the audience interested just by scrolling down the presentation slides. Presentations need to be interactive and animations are great for getting the attention of the audience. Generally, we use animations for slide transitions. Even though presentation tools provide advanced animations, it's our responsibility to choose the animations wisely.

impress.js provides animation effects for moving, rotating, and scaling step transitions. We have to make sure it is used with purpose. Explaining the life cycle of a product or project is an excellent scenario for using rotation animations. So choose the type of animation that suits your presentation contents and topic.

Using themes

Most people like to make the design of their presentation as cool as possible. Sometimes they get carried away and choose from the best themes available in the presentation tool. Themes provided by tools are predefined and designed to suit general purposes. Your presentation might be unique and choosing an existing theme can ruin the uniqueness. The best practice is to create your own themes for your presentations.

impress.js does not come with built-in themes. Hence there is no other option than to create a new theme from scratch. impress.js steps are different to each other unlike standard presentations, so you have the freedom to create a theme or design for each of the steps just by using some simple HTML and CSS code.

Apart from the previous points, we can use typography, images, and videos to create better designs for impress.js presentations. We have covered the background and the importance for impress.js. Now we can move on to creating real presentations using the framework throughout the next few sections.

Downloading and configuring impress.js

You can obtain a copy of the impress.js library by downloading from the github page at https://github.com/bartaz/impress.js/. The downloaded .zip file contains an example demo and necessary styles in addition to the impress.js file. Extract the .zip file on to your hard drive and load the index.html on the browser to see impress.js in action. The folder structure of the downloaded .zip file is as given in the following screenshot:

Configuring impress.js is something you should be able to do quite easily. I'll walk you through the configuration process. First we have to include the impress.js file in the HTML file. It is recommended you load this file as late as possible in your document. Create a basic HTML file called `chapter1.html` and place the following code:

```html
<!doctype html>
<html lang="en">
    <head>
        <title>impress.js </title>
    </head>
    <body>
        <script src="js/impress.js"></script>
    </body>
</html>
```

Downloading the example code

You can download the example code files for all Packt books you have purchased from your account at http://www.packtpub.com. If you purchased this book elsewhere, you can visit http://www.packtpub.com/support and register to have the files e-mailed directly to you.

We have linked the `impress.js` file just before the closing body tag to make sure it is loaded after all the elements in our document. Then we need to initialize the impress library to make the presentations work.

We can place the following code after the `impress.js` file to initialize any existing presentation in the document which is compatible with the impress library:

```html
<script>impress().init();</script>
```

Since we have done the setup of the impress.js library, we can move on to creating our first impressive presentation.

Creating your first presentation

You might be familiar with creating presentations with software tools that provides a slide-by-slide view. Presenting on a web browser is completely different from standard slideshows. We have an infinite space to position the slides in web-based presentations where as we get slide after slide in software-based presentations. Unless we plan the design of the presentations slides in a creative way, we are going have problems using presentations with impress.js.

Get a pencil and paper and design your presentation without using tools on your computer. Using a computer to design will limit our creative thinking capabilities.

Designing the presentation

Let's plan the design for a basic presentation to learn how to use the impress. js library. Once we have the design in mind, it's better to create an outline of the presentation with exact positions of the slides, as shown in the following diagram:

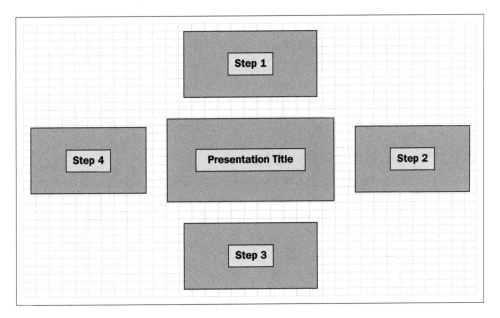

We are going to use five slides for the presentation including the slide with the title. The title of the presentation will be the first slide and it will be placed in the center of the screen. The remaining four slides will be positioned around the first slide at a 90 degree angle allowing the presentation to flow in a circular path. Keeping the design in mind let's start learning about the impress.js elements necessary to create a presentation.

Creating the presentation container

impress.js uses predefined ID's and classes to identify the components in the presentation. Every step of the presentation should be wrapped inside a container with the ID impress and should have a CSS class called step to identify it as a single slide. Here is how a slide will be coded inside the #impress container:

```
<div id="impress">
        <div class="step">Slide Content</div>
</div>
```

We can assign animation effects on each step using HTML data attributes used by impress.js . Here are some of the data attributes supported by impress.js:

- **Positioning**: data-x, data-y, data-z
- **Scaling**: data-scale
- **Rotating**: data-rotate

Creating your first step

The title of the presentation will be the first step of our presentation. According to the design the first step is positioned in the center of the screen and it will be larger than the steps around it. Let's create the first slide using the data attributes mentioned earlier:

```
<div id="impress">
<div id="intro" class="step slide" data-x="-1000"
data-y="-1000" data-scale="3">
    <div><h2 class="title1">Building
    Impressive Presentations</h2>
    <h3 class="title1">with</h3>
    <h3 class="title2">Impress.js</h3>
    </div>
    </div></div>
```

We can assign a unique ID to each step and the ID can be used in the URL to point directly to a specific step. The first slide can be accessed directly by using #/intro. It will default to #/step-N in scenarios where the ID is omitted. Here N is the step number.

The ordering of the steps is important when creating impress.js presentations. The presentation will start with the immediate step element after the #impress container. Therefore, you need to place each step in the order you want it to appear on the presentation.

These steps then need to be positioned in the presentation canvas. Data attributes of impress.js can be defined in the step element. We have used the data-x, data-y, and data-scale attributes for the first slide. We have used -1000 for both data-x and data-y attributes. Hence the first slide will be positioned at -1000 px in the x axis and -1000 px in the y axis in the presentation canvas. impress.js uses the HTML data attributes for adding effects and necessary configurations. You can learn more about HTML5 data attributes at http://www.w3.org/TR/2011/WD-html5-20110525/elements.html.

 It's important to note that impress.js will use the center of the step element for positioning.

Each step can be scaled using the data-scale attribute which is set to 1 by default. This is similar to the *zoom-in* and *zoom-out* features of the web browser. We wanted to make the first step relatively large compared to the other steps. The first step has been scaled three times as compared to the other steps. The next step is going to be on the default scale, so stepping the transition from the first step to the next one can be considered as a *zoom-out* since the steps are scaled from 3 to 1. Scaling from 1 to 3 will provide the *zoom-in* feature when necessary.

Applying styles on steps

The first step has been configured successfully and now we can focus on the contents. These steps are built using HTML elements and hence we can use any design inside the presentation steps. We have separated the presentation title contents into three heading tags with different CSS classes. You also might have noted that we have used another class called slide for the steps. The step class is for identifying the steps in the presentation. Thus we are going to use a different class called slide to specify the common styles for all the steps. Styles can be applied on individual steps by providing CSS for the ID in cases where you need custom styles for specific steps.

A demo presentation provided in the downloaded files contains a stylesheet called `impress-demo.css` for styling the sample presentation. It is not required to use that stylesheet and the creator of impress.js strongly recommends creating your own style files for new presentations.

 impress.js doesn't depend on any external stylesheet. The script adds all the styles it needs for the presentation to work.

First take a look at the demo CSS file to get an idea about how the styles are defined. Then, create a new styles file called `styles.css`. We are going to use common element styles to reset the element styles. Here is how the styles are defined for the `slide` class in our CSS file:

```
.slide {
    display: block;
    width: 1000px;
    height: 700px;
    border-left:25px solid #eee;
    color:#fff;
}
```

Each step has been given a specific width and height to make it consistent. We can design the steps in different sizes unlike most presentation tools. It's up to you to choose the specific dimensions for certain steps. Styles used to design the contents of the first step are self explanatory and anyone with basic CSS knowledge will be able to understand. Look for the `#intro` section in the `styles.css` file for specific styles used for the first step.

Creating Step 1

Step 1 needs to be created after the step with the presentation title. Step 1 is located on top of the title step, so the `data-x` value will remain the same and we need to adjust the `data-y` value to position Step 1.

We had -1000 for the data-y value of the title step. Since we are moving towards the top of screen the y value needs to be decreased. The code for the Step 1 slide with the data-y value of -2500 px will be as follows:

```
<div id="guidelines" class="step slide" data-x="-1000"
data-y="-2500" >
<div class="round"><p>Step 1</p></div>
</div>
```

Apart from the data-x and data-y values, make sure that you include the step class for identifying it as a step, and a slide class for common styles for steps. The rest of the HTML content contains the step data used for the presentation and has no relation with the framework. Custom styles for Step 1 can be found under # guidelines ID of the style.css file.

Creating Step 2

Step 2 is going to be different to the previous step according to our planned design. All the steps apart from the title are placed in a circular path. Rotations can be used to move the steps in a circular path. The contents of Step 2 will be angled by 90 degree to get the circular path. Consider the following code for the Step 2 slide in our design:

```
<div id="graphic" class="step slide" data-x="1000"
data-y="-1500" data-rotate="90">

    <div class="round">Step 2</div>
    </div>
```

Step 2 is positioned to the right of title and the data-x value increases from left to right of your screen. We have thus increased the data-x value from -1000 to 1000. Then we need to rotate the slide by 90 degrees in the slide transition process. impress.js provides the data-rotate attribute to define rotation angles. In this scenario, steps are rotated around the z axis and we can use either data-rotate-z or data-rotate to define the rotations. The rest of the HTML code is the contents of the step and the relative styles can be found in the #graphic section of the style.css file.

The remaining two steps are similar to the step we just discussed. We need to adjust the data-x and data-y values to get the proper placement according to our original design plan.

Limiting the visibility of steps

Generally, all the steps will be positioned relative to each other. Unless we have considerable space between the steps, it is possible to get issues displaying during the presentation. The following screen shows the presentation in the earlier scenario:

We are looking at the first step with the title of the presentation and the contents of other steps which are displayed partially. This is one of the problems we face when positioning steps on an infinite screen and we can solve this issue by using simple CSS codes.

There are some CSS classes assigned to the body element by impress.js during the various processes. Once the presentation is initialized the `impress-enabled` class will be added to the body element. First we hide all the steps by using the following CSS code:

```
.impress-enabled .step {
    margin: 0;
    opacity: 0;
}
```

We have used the `opacity` attribute for hiding the steps in the default view. Alternatively, we can use the `visibility` attribute instead of `opacity`. Setting the margins for steps is optional and you can define your own margin values to suit the presentation. Once the presentation is started, the active step is given a class called `active`. Hence we can display just the active slide and hide all the other steps using the following simple CSS code:

```
.impress-enabled .step.active { opacity: 1;border:none; }
```

Presentation overview

Now we have all the individual styles of the presentation. Creating an overview is very important for the people in the audience as well as for the presenter to know exactly where you are in the presentation. Overview can be considered as a step containing all the other steps. The content of the overview step is intentionally kept blank as follows:

```
<div id="overview" class="step" data-x="-1000" data-y="-1500" data-scale="5"> </div>
```

The impress.js framework allows you to scale steps using the `data-scale` attribute. All the steps apart from the title will be considered scale 1 since we haven't specified the `data-scale` attribute. Overview uses a `data-scale` value of 5 and it will be five times larger than the other steps. When you increase the scale, more detailed information and steps will be displayed on screen.

Consider the following screen for the overview of our presentation:

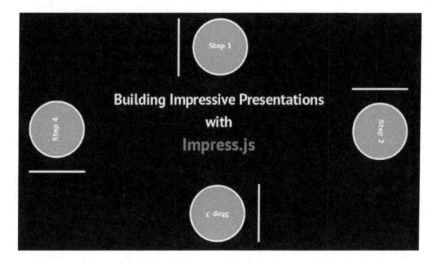

Overview doesn't have any information and shows all the steps in our presentation. We can allow users to click on steps from the overview and directly load the step on the screen. By default, the overview is also considered as a step and it will be clickable. Hence we need to first disable clicking on the overview by hiding it using CSS:

```
#overview { display: none }
```

Now the other steps in overview should be directly accessible. We can enhance the user experience by showing a cursor pointer to the step links using the following code block:

```
.impress-on-overview .step {
    opacity: 1;
    cursor: pointer;
}
```

I have kept the overview step at the end of the presentation for explanation purposes. You can make overview the first slide if necessary.

We now have a completed version of our first impressive presentation. Open the `chapter1.html` file in the web browser and use the arrow keys or *Space* bar to run the presentation. Impress presentations use the complete browser space to run presentations by default. We will be discussing how we can limit the scope of impress presentations to a specific portion of a web page in the upcoming chapters.

Summary

We started this chapter by looking at the background of the impress.js framework and how it was created. Then we talked about the importance of impress.js in creating web-based presentations and various types of usage beyond presentations.

Then we obtained a copy of the framework from the official github page and completed the setup. Finally we created a basic impress.js presentation by explaining the structure of the presentation and effects.

We have covered most of the basics of this framework during the chapter. Now you should be able to create and design a simple presentation using the impress. js framework. In the next chapter, we will be looking at the effects of impress.js in detail and how to combine those effects to produce better presentations.

So stay tuned to create amazing effects with impress.js in the next chapter.

2
Exploring Impress Visualization Effects

In this chapter, we are going to cover the impress.js effects in depth. Effects are the core components in creating impressive visualizations. We are going to use practical examples throughout this chapter to demonstrate the power of effects.

Impress effects are built upon pure CSS transformations, so web designers will find these effects very interesting and easy to understand. Let's get started!

We will be covering the following topics:

- Introduction to CSS transformations
- Positioning effects
- Rotating effects
- Rotations in practice
- Scaling effects
- The importance of positioning in scaling
- Scaling in practice
- Data perspective
- impress.js under the hood

Introduction to CSS transformations

CSS3 provides a wide range of effects for creating animations and working in 3D space. These effects depend on the web browser. Since these effects are still emerging, not all web browsers will have the support for these effects. We need to provide browser-specific syntaxes to make use of these effects. The following is a list of browser prefixes for the most popular browsers:

- **-ms-**: Prefix for Internet Explorer 9
- **-moz-**: Prefix for Firefox
- **-webkit-**: Prefix for Chrome and Safari
- **-o-**: Prefix for Opera

Browser and device support is a key factor in designing impress presentations. impress.js-supported browsers and devices will be discussed in detail in *Chapter 4, Presenting on Different Viewports*.

In the following sections we are going to explore how impress.js uses these CSS transform attributes to generate awesome presentation effects.

Positioning effects

A web browser provides us an infinite canvas to create designs for websites. Usually we choose a specific portion of the browser to design our layouts to be compatible with different screen sizes and viewports. A 960px width grid with unlimited height will be the commonly used approach in web design. This means we are eliminating the possibility of using the space on the top, right, and left sides of our grid. impress. js provides the ability to position elements in a much wider range allowing us to grab the full potential of the browser window.

The amazing thing about impress.js is that we can even position elements in the 3D space using the z index. HTML data attributes are used to specify the positioning information of each step which we are calling slides. The positioning of elements can be done on the x, y, and z axis and we will be looking in depth into all the three directions in the following section.

Positioning on the x axis

We can place the elements in a horizontal direction to use positioning effects on the x axis. Each step in this direction should be assigned with the `data-x` attribute and number of pixels. Once the step transition begins we will be able to see the horizontal sliding effects from the left of our screen to the right, or from the right to the left depending on the values supplied for the `data-x` attribute. The following diagram shows how we can slide in each direction:

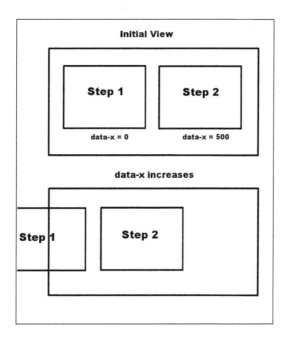

As you can see, the `data-x` value of Step 2 is higher than the `data-x` value of Step 1. The value of `data-x` is increased from left to right and vice versa. Even though there are two steps displayed on screen, we will often design presentations with only one step displayed at any given time. In such scenarios, Step 2 will be hidden in the right section of the screen. On step transition, the x value will increase and Step 2 on the right will slide towards the center of the screen while Step 1 will slide towards the left. Sliding in the opposite direction can be performed by assigning a smaller x value for Step 2.

Steps which have the same x value will overlap each other and will not provide any effect on step transition. Make sure to avoid overlaps when positioning your steps.

Positioning on the y axis

Steps positioned on the y axis are aligned vertically on the screen. The `data-y` attribute is used to define step positions in the vertical direction. On step transition, the vertical sliding effects will be provided from bottom to top or top to bottom depending on the `data-y` values of the presentation steps. The following diagram shows how step transition happens in the vertical direction:

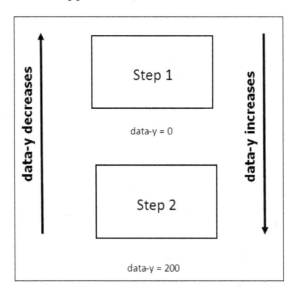

According to the screen, the `data-y` value increases from top to bottom and vice versa. Since Step 2 has a higher `data-y` value, it's positioned below Step 1. When the step transition takes place, subsequent steps will slide from the bottom to top direction of your screen. Sliding in the opposite direction can be performed using a smaller `data-y` value for Step 2.

Positioning on the z axis

Positioning on the z axis can be a difficult task compared to the positioning we did in the previous two sections since we need to think in a 3D perspective. The `data-z` attribute is used to define positions in the z direction. It's best to preview how the steps are positioned in the z axis before we get started. This is shown in the following diagram:

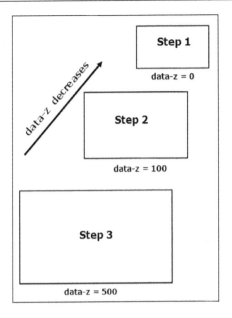

We can see that all the three steps are positioned in the z direction. Step 1 contains the data-z value of 0 and the subsequent steps are given higher data-z values. Although each of the steps is defined with the same dimensions, it seems that the steps are getting larger with the increase in the data-z value.

 In the earlier example, the data-y values are used only for the purpose of preventing an overlap between steps.

Steps with larger data-z values will be closest to the screen while steps with smaller data-z values will be farthest away from the screen. Hence the size of steps differentiates to our eyes. Since the earlier presentation contains larger values for Step 2 and Step 3 , steps will go away from you and you will feel as if you are coming towards the screen. There are two options now for using the data-z attribute, given as follows:

- Keep Step 1 on top: Use lower data-z values for the remaining steps
- Keep Step 1 on bottom: Use higher data-z values for the remaining steps

 impress.js does not provide any restrictions on starting points or positioning elements on the screen. I always prefer using 0 as the value for data attributes of the first slide and assigning minus or plus values depending on the sliding direction I want.

Now you should be able to handle positioning of the elements in impress.js presentations. The real power of impress.js comes when you mix all the effects. Now let's start rotations in the next section. You can use the `data-positioning.html` file in source codes to see how data positioning works.

Rotating effects

In the earlier section, we learned how to use z axis positioning which showed us a glimpse into the 3D world. A real 3D effect comes with *rotations* and *scaling*. impress. js provides rotations around all the three axes, which can be very powerful in designing impressive visualizations. Let's get started on using rotations.

Rotation around the x axis

We can use the `data-rotate-x` attribute to rotate elements around the x axis. The x axis is positioned from the left to the right of your screen in the horizontal direction. Let's take a look at how we can rotate around the x axis using a simple example:

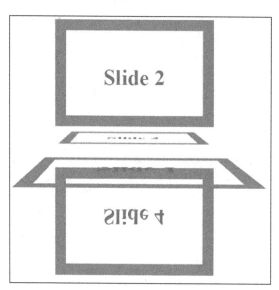

You can see Step 4 rotated around the x axis at a 90 degree angle. The following is the code for this example. You can also work with the `data-rotate-x.html` file in the source code folder for this example.

```
<div id="slide1" class="step slide" data-y="-400"
    data-z="-300" data-rotate-x="90" >
```

```
      <div><h2>Slide 1</h2></div>
</div>
  <div id="slide2" class="step slide"
  data-y="-200" data-rotate-x="180" >
  <div><h2>Slide 2</h2></div>
</div>
  <div id="slide3" class="step slide"
  data-y="-400" data-z="200" data-rotate-x="270" >
  <div><h2>Slide 3</h2></div>
</div>
  <div id="slide4" class="step slide"
  data-y="-600" data-rotate-x="360" >
  <div><h2>Slide 4</h2></div>
</div>
```

Step 2 and Step 4 are completely visible on your screen and the other two steps are partially visible since they are placed at a 180 degree angle to the screen. We have used the data-y and data-z values to position the elements to preview the effects clearly. Using the same positions for steps will result in overlapping. The positive angles are used for the rotations in this example and the rotations will come from the top to the bottom direction of your screen. We can switch the direction of the rotation by assigning negative values for the rotation angles.

Rotation around the y axis

The y axis is positioned from the bottom to the top of your screen. We can use the data-rotate-y attribute to rotate the elements around the y axis. As we mentioned earlier, the positioning of the elements is critical to preview the effect clearly. Rotation around the y axis is shown in the following example:

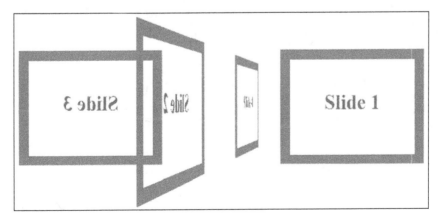

The code for this example is given as follows. It will be similar in nature to the code we used for the x axis. You can also work with the `data-rotate-y.html` file in the source code folder for this example.

```
<div id="slide1" class="step slide" data-x="-600"
data-z="400" data-rotate-y="-90" >
  <div><h2>Slide 1</h2></div>
</div>
<div id="slide2" class="step slide"
data-x="-1000" data-rotate-y="-180" >
  <div><h2>Slide 2</h2></div>
</div>
<div id="slide3" class="step slide"
data-x="-600" data-z="-400" data-rotate-y="-270" >
  <div><h2>Slide 3</h2></div>
</div>
<div id="slide4" class="step slide"
data-x="-200" data-rotate-y="-360" >
  <div><h2>Slide 4</h2></div>
</div>
```

Step 1 and Step 3 will be displayed completely while Step 2 and Step 4 will be partially displayed due to the 180 degree angle around the y axis. We have used negative values for rotation angles in this example, so the rotations will go from left to right in an anticlockwise direction. The rotation direction can be switched by assigning positive values for step angles.

Rotation around the z axis

The z axis is placed into or out of your screen and hence not visible by default. The `data-rotate-z` attribute is used to rotate elements around the z axis. Rotations around the z axis are used in general in our daily web design tasks and will not have any 3D effect like in the previous two examples.

 impress.js provides `data-rotate-z` as the data attribute for rotations around the z axis. We can just use `data-rotate` as the attribute for these rotations since `data-rotate-z` is equal to `data-rotate` in impress.js.

You can take a look at how elements are rotated around the z axis using the following screen. Since this is similar to previous examples I am not going to discuss the codes. You can work with the `data-rotate-z.html` file in the source code folder for this example.

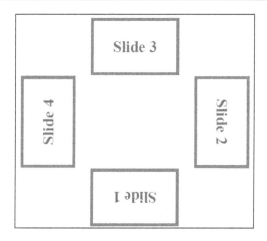

Rotations in practice

Having completed all the rotation techniques in the previous section, we can now move on to creating a practical application using rotations. We will be using rotations around the z axis since it's the most widely used technique. The example application will contain eight circles in a circular path which will be rotated once the presentation starts. Here is a preview of what we are going to develop next:

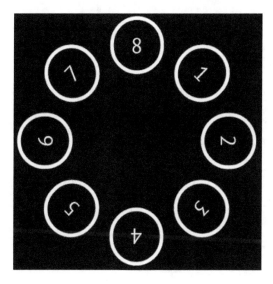

The preceding screenshot shows the overview of our presentation. Let's look at how the first few steps are positioned in the screen using the following code:

```
<div id="slide1" class="step slide" data-x="-100"
   data-rotate-z="45" >
    <span class="circle">1</span>
    <p>Twitter</p>
</div>
<div id="slide2" class="step slide" data-x="-100"
   data-rotate-z="90" >
    <span class="circle">2</span>
    <p>Facebook</p>
</div>
<div id="slide3" class="step slide" data-x="-100"
   data-rotate-z="135" >
    <span class="circle">3</span>
    <p>Linkedin</p>
</div>
```

Each step is positioned at the same x value and z axis rotations are used at 45 degrees angle to each other. Using the same x value allows us to create the circular path for the presentation steps. All the steps are given sequential numbers and some information inside the paragraph tag. I have used popular content sharing sites as the information.

The following code shows the necessary CSS styles for creating circles for the application:

```
.slide .circle {
    border: 10px solid #FFFFFF;
    border-radius: 80px 80px 80px 80px;
    padding: 30px 50px;
    width: 100px;
}
```

We need to make sure that all the information inside the steps is kept hidden by using the following CSS styles:

```
.future p{
    display: none;
}
.past p{
    display: none;
}
```

Steps in impress.js presentations will have a CSS class to define the presentation's status at any given time. The predefined classes will be active , future, and past. We only need the contents of the active step to be visible to the audience. Hence we define the display:none attribute for the paragraph elements of each step which has either a future or past class.

Once the presentation starts, we are going to highlight the number inside the step and make the content of that step visible to the audience. Let's see how our first step looks on the step transition:

The first step number is highlighted and the content is made visible using the active class as follows:

```
.active span{
    background: blue;
}
.active p{
    display: block;
    font-size: 60px;
    margin: 175px 0 20px;
}
```

On each step transition, the active step content will be visible and other step contents will be hidden. This technique can be effectively used to present information about your team, technologies used in your company, or similar concepts. Even though I have only provided the structure for the steps, you can use images and CSS styles to make a cool presentation using these rotation techniques. You can work with the data-rotate-application.html file in the source code folder for this example.

Scaling effects

Scaling in impress.js is much simpler compared to what we discussed in previous sections about positioning and rotations. There is only scaling up or scaling down and the x, y, and z axes will not have any effect on scaling. So let's get things moving by identifying the data attribute for scaling, which will be defined as `data-scale`.

 Scaling up and down can be considered as zoom-out and zoom-in effects. A default `data-scale` value of each step is equal to 1.

Consider the following code snippet, which defines three steps with `data-scale` values:

```
<div id="impress">
    <!-- Row 1 -->
    <div id="slide1" class="step slide"
    data-x="0" data-y="500" data-scale="1" >
        <div><h2>Step 1</h2></div>
    </div>
    <div id="slide2" class="step slide"
    data-x="0" data-y="300" data-scale="2" >
        <div><h2>Step 2</h2></div>
     </div>
     <div id="slide3" class="step slide"
     data-x="0" data-scale="4" >
        <div><h2>Step 3</h2></div>
     </div>
</div>
```

Step 1 has the `data-scale` value of 1 and Step 2 and Step 3 have the `data-scale` values of 2 and 4 respectively. This means, Step 1 will be the smallest and Step 3 will be the largest. Since we have used the same `data-x` value, the center of all the steps will align perfectly. Then we have different values for the `data-y` attribute to display the full contents of the slide without overlapping. Let's see the preview of our three-step presentation.

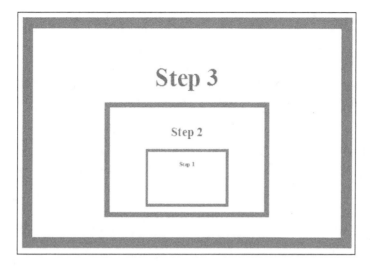

Steps are contained within other steps according to the given positions. Once the presentation starts, Step 1 will display in its full size covering most of the screen and other steps will not be displayed due to its large scale. Then on step transition, Step 1 will go towards the screen with a zoom-out effect and Step 1 will be displayed inside Step 2. This process continues until the presentation completes. You can work with the `data-scale-example1.html` file in the source code folder for this example.

Scaling is not relative to the scaling of other steps. Scaling is purely a higher or lower ratio of its original dimensions. For example, Step 1 and Step 2 having a scale value of 2 does not mean that Step 2 will be twice as large as Step 1. Both steps will be the same size.

The previous example demonstrates the simplest usage of scaling in impress.js. A design like this can be ideal for a presentation with hierarchical data like organizational structures or the layering of components in web application development.

We can begin with the smallest component and go upwards using a higher `data-scale` value or go downwards by beginning with the largest component and using lower `data-scale` values.

The importance of positioning in scaling

Scaling can be used independently without combining other effects. Positioning also makes a huge impact to the meaning of your presentation. In the previous example, the data-x and data-y positions of steps created the hierarchical structure wherein each single step a subcomponent of the next step. The following is a screenshot of the same presentation with slightly different positioning:

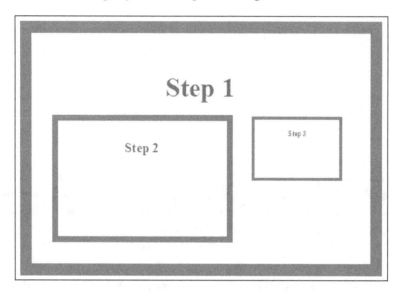

The difference in positioning made Step 2 and Step 3 direct subcomponents of Step 1. This time we are starting big and going smaller into sublevels, which is the opposite of what we did earlier. When the presentation starts we can scale into the subcomponents first and then the subelements will have the sliding effect instead of the scaling effect. You can work with the data-scale-example2.html file in the source code folder for this example.

These types of designs can be used to explain departments of a company and subcomponents of each department.

 Positioning is vital in designing the right kind of presentation to match your concept.

Scaling in practice

In this section, we are going to design a simple presentation to demonstrate scaling in practical scenarios. You must have seen awesome image galleries developed using JavaScript libraries. We can create similar galleries using impress effects with effective usage of the overview of the presentation which we mentioned in *Chapter 1, Getting Started with Impressive Presentations*.

Planning the design

We are going to use 12 image containers for our presentation with three rows and four columns. All the image containers should be visible within the browser window. Once the presentation starts, the first image container should scale up to its full width. Then on the next step transition, we need to go back to the gallery again with the first image highlighted. Then the second container will scale up and continue the process until the presentation is complete.

 Positioning is difficult to manage without an overview. I prefer creating the overview as the first slide and removing it if necessary once the design is completed.

An overview of our image gallery with dummy containers is given. You can work with the `data-scale-application.html` file in the source code folder for this example.

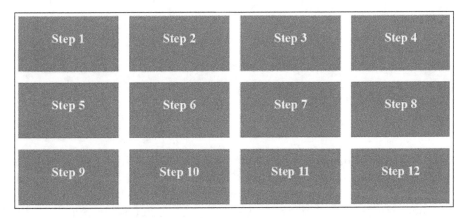

Let's put the overview step into the container with the ID of #impress:

```
<div id="overview" class="step" data-x="2000" data-y="700" data-
scale="3">
 </div>
```

We have used the `data-x` value of 2000 and `data-y` value of 700. These values should be adjusted depending on the positions of our steps to get a perfect overview. We are going to start with the overview and zoom the steps one by one while getting back to the overview. Thus we need an overview step before each of our image step. An overview does not contain any data since it's just used for the purpose of viewing the complete set of steps.

The following code gives you the first row of our image gallery container:

```
<!-- Row 1 -->
<div id="overview" class="step" data-x="2000" data-y="700" data-scale="3">
</div>
<div id="slide1" class="step slide" data-x="0" >
<div><h2>Step 1</h2></div>
</div>
<div id="overview" class="step" data-x="2000" data-y="700" data-scale="3">
</div>
<div id="slide2" class="step slide" data-x="1200" >
<div><h2>Step 2</h2></div>
</div>
<div id="overview" class="step" data-x="2000" data-y="700" data-scale="3">
</div>
<div id="slide3" class="step slide" data-x="2400" >
<div><h2>Step 3</h2></div>
</div>
<div id="overview" class="step" data-x="2000" data-y="700" data-scale="3">
</div>
<div id="slide4" class="step slide" data-x="3600" >
<div><h2>Step 4</h2></div>
</div>
<!-- Row 1 End -->
```

The first row contains the fixed value of 700 for the `data-y` attribute. 1200 is the difference between the `data-x` attributes. The `scale` value will be equal to 1 since we haven't specified a value. In the next row we will change the `data-y` value of steps and keep the same `data-x` values as the first row. Each step is wrapped around the `overview` steps. I have used an ID for the first `overview` element and kept the others blank. You can provide dynamic ID for each overview element when required.

Now we need to highlight the elements which have already been viewed. impress.js provides a class called .past which we can use to develop the highlighting features. Once the step transition is completed, a past class will be implied in the previous step. Now we can define some CSS styles on the .past class to highlight the steps using the following code snippet:

```
.past{
      background:none repeat scroll 0 0 #C54B4B;
}
```

The final output of our image gallery presentation will look as follows when viewed on your browser:

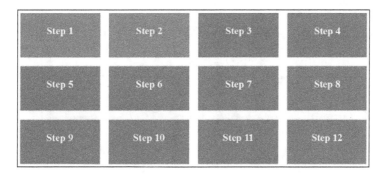

I have given only the structure of elements to keep things simple and make the explanations clear. You can just place images within the step elements to make it an awesome image gallery presentation or any other similar type of presentation.

Data perspective

We have covered all the main effects of impress.js in the previous sections. Finally, we'll take a look at how we can use the data-perspective attribute with impress. js presentations. Perspective determines the distance between you and the z=0 plane. The following is the definition given on CSS perspective by Mozilla.org:

The perspective CSS property determines the distance between the z=0 plane and the user in order to give to the 3D-positioned element some perspective. Each 3D element that is placed between the z=0 and the user is enlarged, each 3D-element with z<0 is shrinked. How much deformation is defined by the value of this property.

As per the definition, the `perspective` attribute will only affect elements in 3D space. impress.js uses `1000` as the default value for the `data-perspective` attribute. You can define higher or lower values to increase or decrease the distance. Let's look at our rotation example in different perspective values to get an idea on how it works. Make sure to define the `data-perspective` attribute on the `#impress` element instead of individual steps as it affects all the steps.

We created an impress rotation example around the y axis in an earlier section. The following screen displays the y axis rotation example with the `data-perspective` value of `500`:

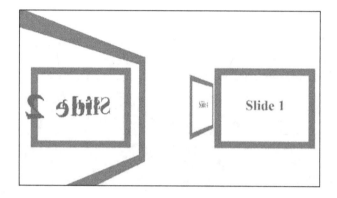

The following screen displays the y axis rotation example with the `data-perspective` value of `1500`:

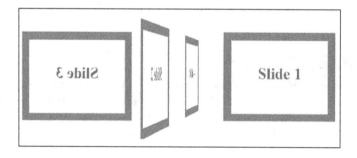

The following screen displays the y axis rotation example with the `data-perspective` value of `3500`:

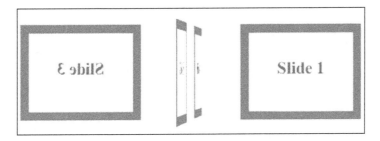

Considering the preceding three screens shown at different `data-perspective` values, we can clearly see that Step 2 and Step 4, which are placed in the z direction, are coming closer to us when the value is decreased and going away from us when the value is increased. Now let's look at how it works on the `data-perspective` value of `0`:

We can see a considerable change in the design when we use a value of `0`. Step 1 and part of Step 2 is displayed and steps in the z direction are completely hidden.

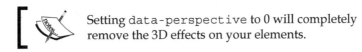

Setting `data-perspective` to 0 will completely remove the 3D effects on your elements.

Make sure you understand how perspective in CSS works before using it in your presentations since it can provide unusual behavior if not used wisely. You can use the `data-perspective.html` file and change the perspective value to see how it works in different scenarios.

impress.js under the hood

We learned how effects in impress work and various kinds of techniques and scenarios. I am sure you would like to explore the core of the impress.js library and learn how these effects really work inside the library, so in this section we'll look at the core code to find the effects.

Once the presentation is loaded on the browser, impress.js will call its `initStep` function to initialize all the steps. The following is the code for the `iniStep` function:

```
var initStep = function ( el, idx ) {
    var data = el.dataset,
        step = {
            translate: {
                x: toNumber(data.x),
                y: toNumber(data.y),
                z: toNumber(data.z)
            },
            rotate: {
                x: toNumber(data.rotateX),
                y: toNumber(data.rotateY),
                z: toNumber(data.rotateZ || data.rotate)
            },
            scale: toNumber(data.scale, 1),
            el: el
        };
    if ( !el.id ) {
        el.id = "step-" + (idx + 1);
    }
    stepsData["impress-" + el.id] = step;
    css(el, {
        position: "absolute",
        transform: "translate(-50%,-50%)" +
                    translate(step.translate) +
                    rotate(step.rotate) +
                    scale(step.scale),
        transformStyle: "preserve-3d"
    });
};
```

All the elements with the `.step` class will be passed to this function. Then the function extracts the values of each `data-attribute` and assigns it to a variable called `step`. Then it will be passed to the CSS function to generate respective CSS styles for the impress effects. The code for the CSS function is as follows:

```
var css = function ( el, props ) {
    var key, pkey;
    for ( key in props ) {
        if ( props.hasOwnProperty(key) ) {
            pkey = pfx(key);
            if ( pkey !== null ) {
                el.style[pkey] = props[key];
            }
        }
    }
    return el;
};
```

The `css` function extracts all the properties from the props variable and calls the `pfx` function to generate browser-specific CSS transformations for the given effects. Once the effects are applied, our step will look like the following code, which uses pure CSS transformations with impress data attributes:

```
<div data-scale="3" data-rotate="90" data-y="-1000" data-x="-1000"
class="step slide active present" id="intro"
style="position: absolute;
-moz-transform: translate(-50%, -50%) translate3d(-1000px, -1000px,
0px) rotateX(0deg) rotateY(0deg) rotateZ(90deg) scale(3);
-moz-transform-style: preserve-3d;">
  </div>
```

Consider the values of the `style` attribute which uses pure CSS transformations. Since I am using Firefox as the browser, the prefix `-moz` is generated. The `data-x` and `data-y` values have been converted as the first two parameters of the `translate3d` function while the `data-rotate` is converted as the `rotateZ` function. Other attributes will also be converted to similar CSS styles when specified.

Having learned impress effects and their usage, now you should be looking at these awesome examples and demos from the official github page for impress.js at `https://github.com/bartaz/impress.js/wiki/Examples-and-demos`.

Summary

Throughout this chapter, we worked with practical examples to explore the impress.js effects and learn the basic syntaxes. In-depth usage of positioning, scaling, and rotations were discussed during this chapter. Finally, we learned how CSS perspective works inside the web browser.

We completed the chapter by looking at the core impress.js code related to generating transform effects. Now you will be able to create impressive effects in your presentations and customize the library code if necessary.

In the next chapter, we are going to dig deeper into the impress code to explore the API functions, events, customizing controls, and configuring of the impress.js library.

3
Diving into the Core of impress.js

The readability and extendibility of impress.js code makes it easy for developers to provide their own implementations of the functions. Although we can use the provided syntax and create impressive visualizations, it is important to dig into the core code and explore the functionalities as developers.

The developer of impress.js wants to keep the library as simple as possible by providing the main presentation creation functionalities. In order to figure out the true potential of the library, we have to take advantage of its open source license and add new functionalities by customizing the core code. Throughout this chapter, we are going to explore the main core functions and see how we can effectively use them to create better presentations.

In this chapter, we are going to cover the following topics:

- impress.js configuration
- Understanding the impress API functions
- Automating presentations
- Creating custom transition timing
- impress.js step events
- How to use the step class
- Working with keyboard configurations
- Assigning custom keys for custom events
- Handling the step click event

Make sure you work with the source code files in order to identify and make customizations to core code as you learn. By the end of this chapter, you will have a proper understanding of how impress.js works inside the core code.

impress.js configuration

We have worked with the default configurations of impress.js up to this point. Generally, these configurations are capable enough to handle any kind of presentation or application created with the library. In certain advanced scenarios, the user might need to alter these configuration options to achieve custom functionality. Hence we are going to cover the default configurations in this section.

Default configurations

Default configurations of the impress library are located in the impress.js file using the defaults variable. The following code shows the default configuration options and their respective values:

```
var defaults = {
      width: 1024,
      height: 768,
      maxScale: 1,
      minScale: 0,
      perspective: 1000,
      transitionDuration: 1000
};
```

Let's get an idea about each of these options in detail:

- width: This option is used to control the width in the window scaling process. This value is converted into pixels through the code. Using a higher value than 1024 will narrow the width of your steps.

- height: This option is used to control the height in the window scaling process. This value is converted into pixels through the code. Using a higher value than 768 will narrow the height of your steps.

- maxScale: This option is used to control the maximum scale in the window scaling process. Reducing this value may change the look and feel of presentation on larger screens.

- minScale: This option is used to control the minimum scale in the window scaling process. Increasing this value may change the look and feel of your presentation on smaller screens.

- perspective: This option defines the distance from the presentation elements with the z axis. Using a value of 0 will prevent any 3D effects in your presentation.

- `transitionDuration`: This option specifies the time between two step transitions. The default value of `1000` means that the steps will be transferred in `1` second. You can increase the value in multiples of 1000 to increase the time duration between steps.

Customizing configurations

Each of these configurations should be defined in the `#impress` presentation container. Using these attributes for the steps will not generate any effect on the presentation. Let's see how we can use these attributes effectively.

Configuring the width and height

We need to use data attributes on the `#impress` element to configure the width and height. `data-width` and `data-height` will be the respective attributes. Consider the following code for the basic configuration of width and height attributes with default values:

```
<div id="impress" data-width="1024" data-height="768"></div>
```

Here is a preview of the screen of a step presentation with the default width and height configurations:

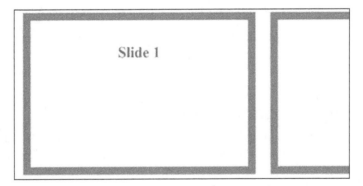

Now we can adjust the width and height and see how it works on different values:

```
<div id="impress" data-width="2048" data-height="1536" ></div>
```

The following is the updated screen of our presentation:

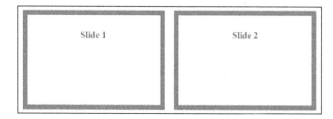

After the modification, the screen has narrowed and you can completely see the second step as well. Thus make sure to use the width and height attributes according to your screen sizes. You can find the example in the `data-width-config.html` file inside source codes.

Configuring the minScale and maxScale

These two properties will also be used in calculations of presentation size according to the window size. `data-min-scale` and `data-max-scale` will be the respective attributes for these properties. The example presentation in the default scaling configurations is given as follows:

```
<div id="impress" data-min-scale="0" data-max-scale="1"  ></div>
```

The presentation layout that will be displayed is similar in nature to the previous screen when the `data-max-scale` is decreased and `data-min-scale` is increased. The working example is located in the `data-scale-config.html` file.

Configuring the perspective

Perspective can be defined using the `data-perspective` attribute. Increasing the value will increase the distance between the elements and the z index and hence the 3D elements will display deeper in the screen. Decreasing the value will reduce the z index and element distance and hence look closer to the screen. Since perspective was explained using examples in *Chapter 2, Exploring Impress Visualization Effects*, I am not going to go into detail here.

Configuring the transition duration

The time between the transitions of two steps can be defined using the `data-transition-duration` attribute on the `#impress` element. The following code shows the `impress` container with a customized transition duration:

```
<div id="impress" data-transition-duration="2000"></div>
```

Make sure you use the proper value for data-transition-duration according to your presentation requirements. Increasing the value too much can cause the presentation to slow down and remove the smoothness in transitions.

Looking at configurations inside the core

Now we have identified the default configuration elements, its purposes and default values, let's see how these values are used inside the library. Once the presentation is started, the impress init function will be called. Inside the function we can find the following code snippet:

```
var rootData = root.dataset;
config = {
    width: toNumber( rootData.width, defaults.width ),
    height: toNumber( rootData.height, defaults.height ),
    maxScale: toNumber( rootData.maxScale, defaults.maxScale ),
    minScale: toNumber( rootData.minScale, defaults.minScale ),
    perspective: toNumber( rootData.perspective,
    defaults.perspective ),
    transitionDuration: toNumber( rootData.transitionDuration,
    defaults.transitionDuration )
};
windowScale = computeWindowScale( config );
```

In the given code, the root will be the #impress element. All the details of the element are passed using root.dataset to the rootData variable. Then each of the configuration options is passed to the toNumber function with a specified value and default value. The following is the implementation of the toNumber function:

```
var toNumber = function (numeric, fallback) {
    return isNaN(numeric) ? (fallback || 0) : Number(numeric);
};
```

The function checks if we have specified a custom numeric value using the isNaN function and returns a default or custom value accordingly. Next, impress passes all the configuration values to the computeWindowScale function using the config variable. computeWindowScale will apply these attributes to the presentation window.

Understanding the impress API functions

impress.js comes up with four useful API functions that can be used to customize the functionality of presenting information in various techniques. We have already worked with the init function throughout the previous chapters. In this section, we are going to focus on three more API functions. Before we dig into the details, let's create an impress object to use API functions, using the following code:

```
var api = impress();
```

We used impress().init throughout the previous chapters to initialize presentations. In order to use API, we need the impress object as given in the preceding code. Once created we can call API methods on the impress object with ease.

The following list contains the impress.js API methods and their respective functionality:

- api.init(): This method initializes the presentation
- api.next(): This method moves to the next step of the presentation
- api.prev(): This method moves to the previous step of the presentation
- api.goto(id): This method moves the presentation to the step given by its index number ID or the DOM element

Inside the next function

The api.next() function moves the steps forward once the presentation starts. Let's see how next works inside the core code function:

```
var next = function () {
    var next = steps.indexOf( activeStep ) + 1;
    next = next < steps.length ? steps[ next ] : steps[ 0 ];

    return goto(next);
};
```

First it gets the active step of the current presentation using the steps array created in the initialization process.

 steps is an array created in the initialization process to store all the elements with the .step class.

Then, it increments the step by 1 and checks whether the current step is the last step on the presentation. Then, it loads the index of the next step or the first step based on the result of the condition check. Finally, it calls the `goto` function with the retrieved index to make the step transition move forward. The `goto` function will be discussed after the next section.

Inside the prev function

The `api.prev()` function moves the steps backwards once the presentation starts. Let's see how `prev` works inside the core code function:

```
var prev = function () {
    var prev = steps.indexOf( activeStep ) - 1;
    prev = prev >= 0 ? steps[ prev ] : steps[ steps.length-1 ];

    return goto(prev);
};
```

The `prev` function works opposite to the `next` function discussed earlier. It retrieves the active step and checks if it's the first step of the presentation. Then, it loads the last step or previous step based on the result of the condition check. Finally, it calls the `goto` function to make the step transition in a backward direction.

Inside the goto function

The `api.goto` function acts as the base for step transition. Both `prev` and `next` functions also use its functionality for navigation between steps. We need to pass the step number or any valid HTML element as the required parameter and a transition time as the optional second parameter. Consider the following example, which calls step number 4 to load in 4 seconds:

```
api.goto(3,4000);
```

> impress.js uses 0 based indices for presentation steps. Therefore we have to pass 3 as the parameter for the `goto` function to get to the fourth step.

Let's see how the `goto` function produces navigation inside the core code function. I am going to filter the navigation-related codes for the explanations to make things clearer:

```
var goto = function ( el, duration ) {
    if ( !initialized || !(el = getStep(el)) ) {
        // presentation not initialized or given
```

```
        element is not a step
        return false;
    }
    window.scrollTo(0, 0);
    // Rest of the code
}
```

The `goto` function accepts the element and duration as the two parameters. Then, it checks whether the presentation is initialized. Next, it uses the `scrollTo` function to traverse to the top page. The necessity of the `scrollTo` function is explained in the code comments ahead.

 Sometimes it's possible to trigger focus on the first link with some keyboard action. The browser, in such a case, tries to scroll the page to make this element visible. (Even that body overflow is set to hidden) and it breaks our careful positioning. So, as a lousy (and lazy) workaround, we will make the page scroll back to the top, whenever the slide is selected.

Now, we'll see how the steps are processed:

```
var step = stepsData["impress-" + el.id];
if ( activeStep ) {
    activeStep.classList.remove("active");
    body.classList.remove("impress-on-" + activeStep.id);
}
el.classList.add("active");
body.classList.add("impress-on-" + el.id);
// Remaining Codes
}
```

First, it checks for an active step and removes the `active` class and other dynamically assigned CSS classes. Then, the `active` class and other dynamic classes are added to the element which is passed as the first parameter to the `goto` function. This is seen in the following code snippet:

```
window.clearTimeout(stepEnterTimeout);
stepEnterTimeout = window.setTimeout(function() {
                onStepEnter(activeStep);
}, duration + delay);
```

In the last part of the function, the code snippet clears the active timeout and creates a function to be executed within the specified delay to make the step transition. Now, we have a basic idea about the functionality of API functions. Let's see how we can use these API functions to make something useful.

Automating presentations

In real life, presentations will be used with manual controlling on most occasions since it is hard to automate presentations with predefined time intervals. You never know how much time it will take to explain a slide and whether the audience will come to you with questions expecting you to answer.

Automating presentations can be used to improve your skills as a presenter. You are not always going to get enough time to do your presentation. Sometimes, you will be bound to deliver the presentation in a limited time period. In such scenarios, you can automate the presentation using certain intervals and try to match the explanations with step transitions to get some practice for a live occasion. Here, we are going to discuss how to use API functions to automate presentations.

The first thing we have to do is create a few steps for the presentation. Since we have already created some presentations, you should be familiar with the syntax. Once the steps are completed we can use simple JavaScript code to automate the presentation. Our script code will look as follows:

```
<script>
    var api = impress();
    api.init();

    $(document).ready(function(){
        var interval = setInterval(function(){
            api.next();
        },5000);
    });
</script>
```

First we create the impress object by calling the `impress()` function. Then, we call `init` on the created object to initialize the presentation. After that we can use the JavaScript `setInterval` function to create repetitive function calling in a given time period. We have used jQuery in this example, but it is not a must. We can just use plain JavaScript code.

Inside the anonymous function, we call the `api.next()` function to make the step transition. In the given scenario, the step transition will happen every 5 seconds in a forward direction. You can try the working examples using the `presentation-automation-next.html` and `presentation-automation-previous.html` files.

Use `api.prev()` inside the anonymous function to automate the step transitions in a backward direction.

In the given scenario, the time limit for each step transition is the same. That's not practical in real scenarios. Some slides need more time while other slides need limited time. So let's see how to address that issue.

Creating custom transition timing

We have to start this process by defining a custom format to store steps and transition durations. We will be using a JavaScript array which looks like the following:

```
var step_transitions = [
            { "slide": 1, "duration":3000 },
            { "slide": 2, "duration":5000 },
            { "slide": 1, "duration":5000 },
            { "slide": 3, "duration":5000 },
    ];
```

We are using **step number** and **duration** between each step transition in the given array. Only a few astute readers will notice that the step numbers are not in order. That means we can use any step number at any given time making the automation **bidirectional** instead of forwards or backwards.

You can create an automated flow of your presentation steps with this technique. Moving forward or backward in any given time is as simple as placing a record in the `step_transitions` array.

Now, let's go through the implementation of this automation technique:

```
$(document).ready(function(){
    var time_frame = 0;
    step_transitions.filter(function (steps) {
            time_frame = time_frame + steps.duration;
            setTimeout(function(){
                    api.goto(steps.slide);
            },time_frame);
    });

});
```

We created a variable called `time_frame` to keep the total time. Then, we used the JavaScript `filter` function to traverse through the array and filter the elements. On each step we added the specified duration for the step from the array to the total time and passed it to the `setTimeout` function. This `setTimeout` function will create timeouts for each step. Then, we used the step number from the `slide` array as the argument for the `goto` function. Once the presentation starts, each step will be called in for a given time period. The process is previewed in the following screenshot:

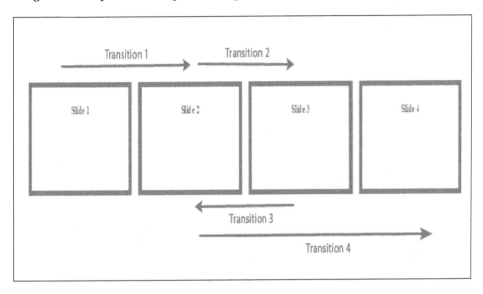

This technique makes it possible to use different transition timings for different steps. The presentation will start from Step 1, moving to Step 2, Step 3, back to Step 2, and finally Step 4 again. You can find the example code for this example in the `presentation-automation-custom.html` file. This technique can be used effectively to create website tours or product tours.

impress.js step events

JavaScript provides a list of in-built events and we can also use event listener functions on those events. Likewise, we can also create our own custom events. impress.js provides two custom events for handling step transition functionality. `stepenter` and `stepleave` is used in the core code to handle these events. Let's take a look at the implementation in the `impress.js` file:

```
root.addEventListener("impress:stepenter", function (event) {
    event.target.classList.remove("past");
    event.target.classList.remove("future");
    event.target.classList.add("present");
```

```
    }, false);

    root.addEventListener("impress:stepleave", function (event) {
        event.target.classList.remove("present");
        event.target.classList.add("past");
    }, false);
```

In each step transition, the stepleave event of the current step is fired first, followed by the stepenter event of the next step. Inside the stepenter event, we remove the past and future classes and add the present class to make it an active step. In the stepleave event we remove the present class and add the past class to define it as already viewed.

The impress step classes are detailed as follows:

- future: These steps are not displayed yet
- past: These steps are already displayed
- present: This step is displayed currently in the presentation

We can use these custom impress events to provide our own functionality without modifying the core library code. Here is how the customizations are done inside your HTML file:

```
<script>
    $(document).ready(function(){
        document.addEventListener
        ("impress:stepenter", function (event) {
            // Code for step enter
        }, false);

        document.addEventListener
        ("impress:stepleave", function (event) {
            // Code for step leave
        }, false);
    });
</script>
```

Inside the HTML file, add the two events as given in the example and create custom code inside the function. This functionality is suitable for changing the CSS styles of steps dynamically through the presentation.

How to use the step class

impress.js uses the step class to identify an item as a step in the presentation and apply necessary effects. At any given stage, each step has one of the three classes present, past, or future. In the previous chapters, we learned how to use these classes to provide custom functionality. Now we are going to look at the life cycle of a step using these three classes.

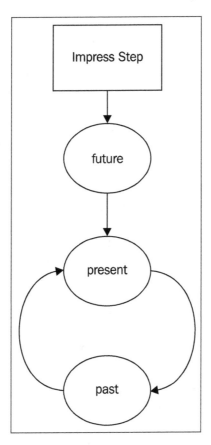

Each step on the impress presentation is given the class future on initialization. When the step becomes the current active step, the present class will be assigned and the future class will be removed. In the next step transition, the current step is assigned the class past and next step becomes present. After that the last step presentation will start again from the beginning and present class will be assigned. This cycle continues until you stop the presentation.

The step will have the future class only once throughout the presentation. Even if you run the presentation multiple times, the future class will not be assigned after the first cycle. From the second cycle onwards, the step will switch between the past and present classes.

Working with keyboard configurations

Having control over your presentation is essential in situations where we have time constraints for completing the presentation. We can either choose to run the presentation manually or automatically as we did in the previous section. In either case, control options play a vital role. impress.js comes in with in-built key configurations for controlling the presentation. Throughout this section, we will be covering default impress keys and how to configure your own for custom functionality.

Default keyboard configurations

The main functionality of any presentation is to step forward or backward. Impress uses *Tab*, the Space bar, *Page Down*, the down arrow, and the right arrow as the keys for navigating forward. Backward navigation is done using *Page Up*, the left arrow, and the up arrow keys. Let's see how keyboard configurations are created inside the code.

Inside the impress core

Keyboard configurations are created inside the impress.js file but first we'll take a look at how the default functionality of keys is prevented using the following code:

```
document.addEventListener("keydown", function ( event ) {
    if ( event.keyCode === 9 || ( event.keyCode >= 32
    && event.keyCode <= 34 ) || (event.keyCode >= 37
    && event.keyCode <= 40) ) {
        event.preventDefault();
    }
}, false);
```

Each key in the keyboard has a default functionality. For example, the Space bar will create spaces and *Tab* will create tabs. First, we need to disable the default functionality to make these keys available for the functions of our application. We can use the preventDefault method of the keydown event to disable the default functionality. Now, in the following code, we can see how default configurations for functions are done inside the core code:

```
document.addEventListener("keyup", function ( event ) {
    if ( event.keyCode === 9 || ( event.keyCode >= 32
    && event.keyCode <= 34 ) || (event.keyCode >= 37
    && event.keyCode <= 40) ) {
        switch( event.keyCode ) {
            case 33: // pg up
            case 37: // left
            case 38: // up
                    api.prev();
                    break;
            case 9:  // tab
            case 32: // space
            case 34: // pg down
            case 39: // right
            case 40: // down
                    api.next();
                    break;
        }

        event.preventDefault();
    }
}, false);
```

First we check for the pushed key using `keyCode` of the event. The key code of each assigned key is included inside the `if` statement. Then we assign *Page Up*, and the left and up arrows to the `prev` function using the `switch` statement. The `api.prev()` function is called on specified keys. Similarly, we assign *Page Down*, *Tab*, the Space bar, and the right and down arrow keys for the `api.next()` function.

Using the arrow keys, the *Page Up*, *Page Down* buttons, and, Space bar is quite common in presentation navigation, but using the *Tab* key for navigation is an uncommon technique. There is a special reason for choosing the *Tab* key. Let's see what Bartek Szopka says about choosing the *Tab* key:

> *This one is quite controversial, but the reason it ended up on this list is quite an interesting story... Remember that strange part in the impress.js code where window is scrolled to 0,0 on every presentation step, because sometimes browser scrolls viewport because of the focused element? Well, the [tab] key by default navigates around focusable elements, so clicking it very often caused scrolling to focused element and breaking impress.js positioning.*

> *I didn't want to just prevent this default action, so I used [tab] as another way to moving to next step... And yes, I know that for the sake of consistency I should add [shift+tab] as opposite action...*

Assigning custom keys for custom events

We might not be familiar with the default keys used for impress presentations. In such cases, we can assign our own keys for existing functions and new keys for new functions. Let's see how we can modify the code to add new keys to existing functionalities. Let's add the letter *p* for previous and *n* for next.

```
document.addEventListener("keyup", function ( event ) {
    if ( event.keyCode === 9 || ( event.keyCode >= 32
    && event.keyCode <= 34 ) || (event.keyCode >= 37
    && event.keyCode <= 40) || event.keyCode === 78 ||
    event.keyCode === 80  ) {
        switch( event.keyCode ) {
            case 80: // letter p

            // key codes for default previous keys
                    api.prev();
                    break;
            case 78:  // letter n

            // key codes for default next keys
                    api.next();
                    break;
        }
```

Each key in the keyboard has a specific character code. First, we have to find the character code, also known as the key code, of the keys we want to assign into our impress presentation. We can find these character codes by searching for *JavaScript Char Codes* in a search engine. Once we get the specific key codes for the letters *p* and *n*, add it to the switch statement, as highlighted in the code, to assign the keys. Then, modify the if statement on top of the switch statement to add the new keys. Also, you have to add those key codes into the keydown event to prevent any default behavior.

Adding new keys for new events

We can create new functions and assign custom keys to impress presentations by modifying the existing switch statement. Earlier, I mentioned the necessity for having an overview step. We'll just add the letter *o* as the key for the overview step. The implementation for the overview step keys will look as follows:

```
case 79:
        var overview_step  = document.
        getElementById("overview");
        api.goto(overview_step);
        break;
```

First, we have to find the overview of the presentation using its ID. `79` will be the key code for the letter *o*. We assume that `#overview` will be used for the overview step of any presentation. Once we get the element, we can use the `goto` function to directly traverse to the overview slide.

Now, let's create two new functions to traverse to the first and last slide of the presentation, using the following code snippet:

```
case 70:
    api.goto(0);
    break;

case 76:
    api.goto(-1);
    break;
```

In the code given, `70` and `76` will be the key codes of letters *f* and *l* respectively. Impress presentations has a zero-based index. Hence we can traverse to the first step by using the index `0` on the `goto` function. Similarly, we can use the index `-1` to traverse to the last step. It's important to note that all the new keys used inside the `switch` statement need to be added to the `if` statement and `keydown` event.

impress.js provides a simplified method for assigning keys to new functionalities. Make sure you customize and add new keys in your own presentations. You can work with the `keyboard.html` file and `impress-keyboard.js` files for examples in this section.

Handling the step click event

Apart from the keys discussed in the previous section, impress.js provides a `click` event on each step. We can directly move to any step by clicking on the step.

> Ideally we should see more than one slide to use the `click` event. Generally, we will have steps covering the complete width and height of the screen, so we can only use `click` event in an overview step for most cases.

Let's see how the `click` event is handled inside the core impress code:

```
document.addEventListener("click", function ( event ) {
    var target = event.target;
    // find closest step element that is not active
    while ( !(target.classList.contains("step") && !target.classList.
contains("active")) &&
        (target !== document.documentElement) ) {
        target = target.parentNode;
    }

    if ( api.goto(target) ) {
        event.preventDefault();
    }
}, false);
```

This code first gets the target element on the `click` event. Then, it checks if it contains the `step` class to make sure it is an actual step in the presentation. Next, it checks if the target is the current step using the active class. Then, it traverses to the target element using the `goto` function.

Now we have covered all the necessary details for working with impress core code.

Summary

impress.js provides well organized source code for customizing existing functionalities and extending core functionalities by adding new sections. Default configuration options are provided for general purpose usage. Customizations can be made to default configurations to suit your needs.

The library is built upon four simplified API functions for presentation, initialization, and transition. We can take advantage of the API functions by specifying and calling them in our own code to provide custom behaviors, such as automating presentations.

Step transitions are build upon well organized processes using CSS classes. Each step, at any given time, is given a specific state and it can be used to add different behaviors to presentations.

Finally, we discussed keyboard configurations and managing your own keys for impress functions. Before moving on to the next chapter, I recommend you work with demo files and understand the core concepts properly.

In the next chapter, we are going to look at handling impress presentations in different viewports including mobile devices. So stay tuned for a chapter full of excitement.

4
Presenting on Different Viewports

Presentations used to be created and run fullscreen. Even though impress.js was built to create presentations, there are various other implementations for it. It's thus necessary to learn the viewports and devices to take advantage of all the features in impress.js.

We used fullscreen presentations throughout the previous chapters. In this chapter, we are going to look at how to use impress.js inside a container. Finally, we are going to see the compatibility of impress.js in mobile and tablet devices.

In this chapter, we are going to cover the following topics:

* Fullscreen presentations
* Using impress.js inside a container
* Developing a content slider
* impress.js presentations on mobile devices
* Issues in designing for mobile devices
* Best design practices for mobiles devices

Fullscreen presentations

We have created presentations utilizing the full browser width and height throughout this book. This is the default behavior of the impress.js library. On one hand we have the advantage of designing in a larger viewport inside the infinite canvas, and on the other a visible portion of the presentation design varies based on your screen size. So it's hard to control the visible area with different screen sizes.

Designing for fullscreen or designing inside a specified container depends on your requirements. The following are some of the practical usages of fullscreen presentations:

- Slide presentations
- Single page websites

Using impress.js inside a container

Designing inside a container is much easier compared to fullscreen presentations since we have full control over the visible area. This is a very useful technique when using impress.js, different from its default functionality.

The following are some of the practical usages of impress.js inside a specific container:

- Image galleries
- Content sliders
- Personal portfolios

We will be creating a content slider to learn how impress.js works inside a specified container.

Developing a content slider

Content sliders are very popular components in website design. Most websites have a slider on the homepage to highlight important content within a limited space. impress.js is developed in a way that we can add new custom functionality with ease. Presentations can easily be converted to content sliders with minimum customizations.

Throughout the next section, we are going to build a fully functional content slider from scratch.

Planning the design

Sliders contain steps with HTML contents. This is similar to what we did in previous presentations. But this time, the slider will be created inside a container with predefined dimensions instead of fullscreen. Let's now take a look at the common functionalities of a slider before we get started:

- Slides play automatically
- Navigation controls for previous and next slides

- Play/pause functionality
- Slide numbers for direct traversing
- Highlights the active slide number

Here is a preview of the slider we are going to develop in this section:

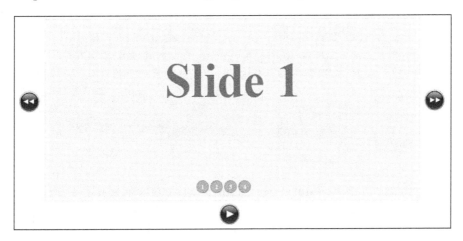

Designing slides

The first step is to add the steps to the #impress element and initialize the library. I'll be using basic content for these steps. Feel free to add real content and styles with CSS using the source file slider.html:

```html
<div id="impress">
    <div id="slide1" class="step slide" data-x="640"
    data-y='440'    >
        <div><h2>Slide 1</h2></div>
    </div>
    <div id="slide2" class="step slide" data-x="-2500"
    data-y='-1200' data-rotate="60"   >
        <div><h2>Slide 2</h2></div>
    </div>
    <div id="slide3" class="step slide" data-x="2500"
    data-y='1200' data-z='200'   >
        <div><h2>Slide 3</h2></div>
    </div>
    <div id="slide4" class="step slide" data-x="2500"
    data-y='1200'  data-z='1500'   >
        <div><h2>Slide 4</h2></div>
    </div>
</div>
```

We have four slides with simple content inside the #impress element. Initialize the library by assigning the impress object to a variable, as we did in *Chapter 3, Diving into the Core of impress.js*. We haven't done anything new yet. So the presentation will be shown in fullscreen.

Wrapping the presentation inside a container

Now we have to restrict the presentation area for the slider by wrapping the presentation inside a specific container. Create a new element with the ID #wrap and place the #impress element inside it, as shown in the following code snippet:

```
<div id="wrap">
        <div id="impress">
        // Content for steps
        </div>
</div>
```

Once inserted, use the following styles on the #wrap element to make the presentation limited to a certain area of the browser instead of the full screen:

```
#wrap{
    background: none repeat scroll 0 0 #EEEEEE;
    border: 10px solid #F8F8F8;
    border-radius: 10px 10px 10px 10px;
    height: 460px;
    margin: 20px auto;
    outline: 1px solid #cfcfcf;
    overflow: hidden;
    position: relative;
    width: 900px;
}
```

The presentation is limited to a specific area by providing a fixed width and height for the wrapper element. overflow: hidden allows us to hide elements beyond the scope of the visible area to avoid generating unnecessary scrollbars. Now the presentation will be center aligned on your screen with limited dimensions and will look similar to the other JavaScript sliders. Let's create the slider functionalities.

Playing the slider automatically

Generally, the slider should play automatically once the page is loaded. This is not a new functionality since we implemented it in the previous chapter. We are going to use jQuery to support DOM manipulation. Let's take a look at the code for auto playing. It is as simple as using the api.next() function inside the JavaScript's setInterval function.

```
$(document).ready(function(){
    interval = setInterval(function(){
            api.next();
        },3000);
});
```

Creating navigation controls

Most sliders will have previous and next buttons for traversing to the adjacent slides. We are going to use these navigation buttons outside the slider. You can place it inside according to your preferences. First we have to create the buttons for navigation as follows:

```
<div class="navigation">
    <a href="javascript:void(0);"  class="prev-btn" >
    <img src="images/Aqua-Previous-icon.png" /></a>
    <a href="javascript:void(0);"  class="next-btn" >
    <img src="images/Aqua-Next-icon.png" /></a>
</div>
```

Add this code snippet right after the #wrap container. Once the button is clicked, the respective jQuery function will be called to traverse to the adjacent slide, as shown in the following code:

```
$("body").on("click", ".prev-btn", function(){
    api.prev();
});
$("body").on("click", ".next-btn", function(){
    api.next();
});
```

The custom function used here will call the next and previous functions of the impress.js API using the impress object generated in the initialization. Now you should be able to use these navigation buttons to access adjacent slides.

Creating the play/pause features

Ideally, we should have the facility to pause the slider and play the slider at any given time. First, we have to define a button to provide play/pause functionality. Add the following code after the navigation element to create the play/pause buttons:

```
<div id="play-pause" class="play-pause pause-btn" >
  <img src="images/Aqua-Pause-icon.png" />
</div>
```

Initially, the pause button is displayed since the presentation has already started. the CSS class pause-btn is used to display and handle the pause functionality. Similarly, play-btn will be used to handle play functionality. Consider the implementation of these buttons:

```
$("body").on("click", ".pause-btn", function(){

    $(this).addClass("play-btn");
    $(this).removeClass("pause-btn");
    $("#play-pause").find("img").attr("src",
    "images/Aqua-Play-icon.png");
    clearInterval(interval);
});
```

First, we assign the jQuery live click event to the pause button. Once the button is clicked we remove the CSS class for the pause button and add the class for the play button. Then, we change the image of the button according to play/pause functionality. Finally, we clear the automatic playing of the slider using the clearInterval function to pause the slider.

Similarly, we can handle the play functionality using the following code:

```
$("body").on("click", ".play-btn", function(){
    $(this).addClass("pause-btn");
    $(this).removeClass("play-btn");
    $("#play-pause").find("img").attr("src",
    "images/Aqua-Pause-icon.png");

    interval = setInterval(function(){
        api.next();
    },3000);
});
```

Most of the code is similar to the pause button handling code. For the play button, we need to use the setInterval function instead of clearInterval to keep the presentation moving to the next step. Now you have the capability of playing and pausing the slider at any given time.

Adding slide numbers

Sliders generally contain pagination like navigation to traverse directly to any given slide. Some sliders use dots or circles while other slides use numbered navigation buttons. We will be using numbered buttons inside the slider. Let's add the numbered buttons to the slider.

```
<div class="pagination"></div>
```

We are going to generate numbered buttons dynamically instead of hard coding in the file. So we just need to add a container with the class `pagination`, after the `#impress` element. Now we'll go to the implementation of numbered buttons.

```
var length = $(".step").length;
for(i=0;i<length;i++){
    $(".pagination").append("<div class='page-num
    pag-slide"+(i+1)+"' onclick='api.goto("+i+")'
    >"+(i+1)+"</div>");
}
```

Initially, we calculate the number of steps on the page load. Then, we assign a button with a dynamic sequential number while traversing through each step. We call the `goto` function of the API, once the user clicks on the number.

Highlighting the active slide

Since I have used content such as Slide 1, Slide 2, we know which one is the current slide. When the real content is used there will not be any numbers on the slides, so we should have a method of identifying the current slide. We can highlight the active slide to provide this feature. Consider the following code:

```
document.addEventListener("impress:stepenter",
function (event) {
    var page_step = $(".active").attr("id");
    $(".pagination").find(".pag-"+page_step).
    addClass("active-bullet");
}, false);

document.addEventListener("impress:stepleave",
function (event) {
    $(".pagination").find(".page-num").
    removeClass("active-bullet");

}, false);
```

We can use `stepenter` and `stepleave` events to create the highlighting functionality. On `stepenter` we find the active slide using the `active` class that assigns a new class called `active-bullet` to highlight the current slide number. Similarly, we remove the `active-bullet` from the current step on step leave event.

Now we have completed developing the slider with impress.js. You should have a fully functional slider ready to use in your application. Try adding your own customizations to make it more attractive.

impress.js presentations on mobile devices

Impress is widely used as a presentation creation library. Presentations are created using laptops or desktop computers in common scenarios, but it is a common technique to embed presentations inside web pages, so mobile device users should be able to view the presentations without issues.

The impress.js library was originally built to work with web browsers which support CSS transforms. Hence it doesn't work on most of the mobile device browsers which do not have support for CSS transform capabilities.

 Even though impress presentations will not work on most mobile devices, iPad and iPhone devices provide support for its features and animations. New versions of browsers are released regularly to provide more features. Hence we can expect more browsers to support impress presentations in the near future.

In scenarios where we use impress.js as embedded presentations, compatibility with mobile devices has to be considered and the design should be adjusted.

 Unfortunately, we don't have a workaround for applications such as sliders, galleries, and single page websites in mobile devices due to the higher usage of custom functionality and impress effects.

Issues in designing for mobile devices

Basically, we have to provide an information message to the user in scenarios where the browser doesn't have the support for impress.js functionality. This is handled by the core code inside the library. Handling browser fallback methods and customizations will be discussed in *Chapter 6, Troubleshooting*.

Providing a fallback message doesn't mean we are done with handling impress.js for mobiles. Effects such as scaling, transforms, and rotations might not work on those devices. Still, the user should be able to read the whole content of the presentation without encountering any issues.

Let's go through some impress.js presentations on mobile devices to figure out the common problems in designing for mobiles.

Scenario 1

The images shown here are taken from a presentation in the demo section of the impress.js github page. Obviously, it is being designed for impress-supported browsers. You can take a look at the presentation at `http://johnpolacek.github.com/WhatTheHeckIsResponsiveWebDesign-impressjs/`.

The following is a screenshot from the sample impress presentation on supported browsers:

The following screenshot shows the same presentation on unsupported browsers:

This presentation works perfectly in supported browsers. It uses CSS opacity to reduce the visibility initially. Then the opacity is increased on step transition to highlight the content.

Since step transition doesn't work on unsupported browsers, content will be displayed with very low opacity which makes the content almost unreadable to mobile users. If you are using CSS on step transitions, make sure it doesn't affect the mobile users.

Scenario 2

In this scenario, we are going to take a look at another presentation in the impress. js demo section on github. The following screenshot shows the presentation on supported browsers:

Now let's take a look at the same presentation in an unsupported browser using the following screenshot:

In this scenario, the web interface which supports impress.js provides an unclear interface to the users while the mobile interface looks much more organized and readable. This is because the steps are placed in the limited x, y range, so some steps overlap others. Make sure you check your presentation in both supported and unsupported browsers while designing.

Scenario 3

In *Chapter 2, Exploring Impress Visualization Effects*, we talked about adding meaning into your presentation using the proper design. We created a presentation with steps inside other steps to show hierarchal data representations. Let's see how it works on supported browsers on mobile devices.

The following screenshot shows the presentation in supported browsers:

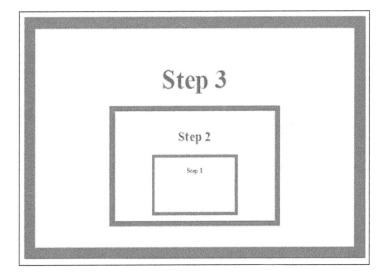

The following screenshot shows the same presentation on unsupported browsers and devices:

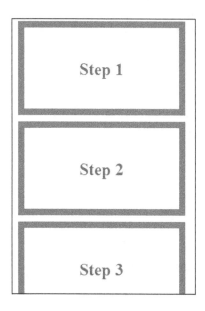

We can see that the steps are displayed under the previous step instead of being inside Step 3. This means the hierarchal structure is not visible in mobile devices. If you are adding meaning to your presentations through design, make sure it is not mandatory in understanding the presentation since mobile users will have issues in such cases.

Now you should have a clear understanding of how impress.js works in unsupported browsers. It's your responsibility to plan the design wisely.

Best design practices for mobiles devices

There are no recommended methods or best practices for designing for mobile devices since most developers are still using impress.js as a presentation tool. Ideally, you should be getting this knowledge by designing as many presentations as you can. I'll list down some of the common mistakes to avoid when designing for mobiles.

- Limit the dynamic CSS on the `stepenter` and `stepleave` events
- Don't hide the steps on the initial page load
- Position elements properly to avoid the overlapping of steps
- Don't rely on effects to provide meaning to presentations

The guidelines mentioned in this section don't guarantee that your presentation will look better in unsupported browsers for all possible scenarios. We can look for an alternative approach of using CSS media queries to handle unsupported browsers.

In this technique, you will have to create a separate design for unsupported devices, inside another container. Once impress.js recognizes an unsupported browser, you can hide the impress presentation container and display the mobile-specific design. CSS media queries can be used effectively to handle the dimensions of mobile devices.

Implementing a mobile-specific layout is beyond the scope of this book. You should look to learn responsive web design if you are willing to learn more about how to handle mobile device layouts.

Summary

impress.js allows you to create presentations in full dimensions of the browser window as well as inside a container with specific dimensions.

Since impress uses CSS transforms to create effects, most mobile browsers will not support presentations created with the library. We should consider both supported and unsupported browsers in designing presentations to provide a better experience for users browsing from all kinds of devices.

We have to create adaptable designs by simplifying the step transitions and continuous testing on different browsers and devices.

In the next chapter, we are going to build a fully functional single page website using the theories and techniques we learned in the previous chapters. Until then, make sure you try out all the examples given in the source code.

Creating Personal Websites

5

The internet is full of websites with amazing designs. As a web developer and designer, there's nothing better than creating your own website to impress your clients and friends. impress.js can be used effectively to create a complete website with amazing effects. Apart from normal click-based navigation, you can use keyboard controls to navigate through any part of the website.

We are going to create a fully functional website with different types of effects to match different types of data in your profile. Once you understand the process, you will be able to create new types of websites for different clients within a few minutes of using impress.js.

Let's get started!

In this chapter, we are going to cover the following topics:

- Planning the website structure
- Creating pages
- Designing the home page
- Designing the portfolio page
- Designing the timeline page
- Defining the timeline navigation
- Designing the services page
- Handling the navigation menu
- Creating the navigation hint

In this chapter, we are going to use the jQuery library for adding custom functionality to the impress.js presentation. I encourage you to learn the basics of jQuery in order to understand the single page website creation process.

Planning the website structure

Personal websites are essential for showing your skills and improving your reputation online. Earlier people used to create websites with a bunch of HTML pages. These days single page websites are becoming very popular. You can find various free plugins for creating such websites without putting in much effort.

impress.js can be extended to create single page websites. Actually, we are going to create a presentation in a way that makes it look like a real website. Before we move any further, let's plan the structure of the website.

The sketch of the structure of our website is shown as follows:

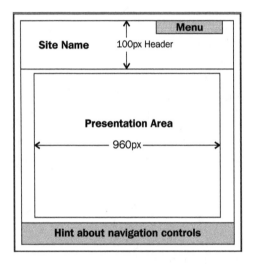

Generally, all web pages have a header with a navigation menu, so we are going to use a fixed header with the name of the site and the navigation menu. It's important to know that the header is not a part of the impress.js presentation. After the header, we place the steps of the presentation to look like real web pages. A 960px container has been chosen for the content as it's the most popular grid size in web design.

Designing the header

impress.js presentations use the full screen width and height of the web browser ; this means that the step data could show on top of the header section, so we have to consider the height of the header when designing presentation steps. Let's look at the HTML code for the header section and the necessary CSS styles:

```
<div id="header">
    <div id="header_panel">
```

```
        <h1 class="site_name">JOHN DOE</h1>
        <div class="top_menu">
            <ul>
                <li id="menu-about" >
                <a href="#/about">Home</a></li>
                <li id="menu-portfolio-overview" >
                <a href="#/portfolio-overview">Protfolio</a></li>
                <li id="menu-timeline-start" >
                <a href="#/timeline-start">Timeline</a></li>
                <li id="menu-services-overview" >
                <a href="#/services-overview">Services</a></li>
            </ul>
        </div>
    </div>
</div>
```

Inside the header, we have the title and list of menu items for the pages. I have used the div element to create the header section. Instead, you can use the HTML5 header element to design the header, if necessary. In the code given, the navigation menu is defined as a static menu where we need to insert the element manually. Later in this chapter, I'll show you how to make it work using step events and links.

Here are the necessary styles for the header:

```
#header{
    background: #f8f8f8;
    height: 100px;
    border-top: 5px solid #D00505;
}
```

The height of the header is the important factor here. The header takes 100px as the height. Now let's see how to avoid conflicts between the step data and header.

Creating the presentation wrapper

As I mentioned previously, we have to limit the scope of the presentation display area using a wrapper. You should be familiar with this technique since we used it in the previous chapter for creating the slider. Let's create the wrapper.

Here is the HTML code for the wrapper:

```
<div id="wrap">
    // Impress presentation will be located here
</div>
```

We have to avoid the conflicts by defining necessary styles, as follows:

```
#wrap{
    min-height: 400px;
    margin: 20px auto;
    overflow: hidden;
    position: relative;
    width: 960px;
}
```

We need to define the height and width of the wrapper and set `overflow` to `hidden` to hide the unnecessary elements of other pages. Relative positioning allows us to clear the conflicts with the header section. Now the wrapper will start right after the header is finished. We are ready to create the pages of our site.

Creating pages

We will be creating a simple website with four pages in this chapter. The whole site will act as a single impress presentation. Each one of the pages will be a step or collection of steps inside the presentation. Let's look at the pages we are going to create:

- **Home page**: This page contains an introduction about you
- **Portfolio pages**: This page contains your work samples
- **Timeline**: This page contains benchmarks of your career
- **Services page**: This page contains all your services

 The unique thing about building websites with impress.js is that users can use keyboard navigation as well as common navigation controls.

Designing the home page

On the home page, we are going to show the details about you. It consists of multiple steps with text-based content for the most part. Previously, we created large steps which took the full screen or scope of the presentation, but now we are planning to do something different by creating multiple small steps which are visible in the browser screen at the same time, using CSS to handle the step transition. The following is a preview of our home page:

The content shown in this screenshot will be the first step of the website. After the first step, we have a few text-based smaller steps that are used to show the details of the owner of website. Let's now take a look at how the steps are placed inside the presentation:

```
<div id="impress">
    <div id="about" class="step slide" data-x="0" data-y='0'  >
        // First step Data
    </div>

    <div id="slide2" class="step slide" data-x="0" data-y='500' >
        <div class="intro-title">Web Developer</div>
    </div>

    <div id="slide3" class="step slide" data-x="0" data-y='600'    >
        <div class="intro-title">from Australia </div>
    </div>
</div>
```

Step 1 is located at the coordinates of 0,0. All the other text slides on the home page need to be placed under the first step. We have used 500 for the data-y attribute of the second step and each of the subsequent steps are placed within a margin of *100* in the *y* direction. Only two of the text steps are shown here. You can add as many steps as you want with proper margins. The following is a preview of the text images in the default context:

We can see that all the steps look similar to each other. Instead, we want to show the active step highlighted from the rest of the steps. Impress classes for the status of the step can be used easily to create this functionality. Text steps contain a class called intro-title which will come handy in this scenario. CSS opacity will be used to provide the highlighting effect. Consider the following code:

```
.past .intro-title{
    opacity:0.1;
}
.future .intro-title{
    opacity:0.1;
}
.active .intro-title{
    opacity:1;
    text-transform: uppercase;
}
```

The active step contains the class active while all other steps contain either the past or future class. We reduce the text opacity of the past and future classes to make them almost invisible. In the active class an opacity of 1 is used to make it completely visible. Also, we are transforming the text to uppercase in step transition as an additional feature. Once the styles are applied, the text steps will look like the following:

Designing the portfolio page

We create personal websites to expose our skills to the world. On the home page, we give a brief introduction about us and what we actually do. But no one is going to believe you unless you can provide facts that prove the given details. Providing examples of our work is the best way to convince the readers of your website or potential clients. So let's start creating a cool portfolio page.

There are two types of pages we need for designing our portfolio:

- **Portfolio gallery**: This page contains a collection of work samples
- **Portfolio single**: This page contains detailed information about a single work sample

Portfolio gallery

We are going to create a separate step for each of the portfolio items. We can use an overview step with a larger scale to show the portfolio steps as a gallery. Let's create the portfolio overview step:

```
<div id="portfolio-overview" class="step slide" data-x="3250"
data-y='400'
data-scale="3.5" data-type="portfolio-gallery" >
</div>
```

Positioning and scaling are the two most important factors in designing proper overviews of your presentation. Here we have used 3250 for the data-x attribute. Thus the portfolio items are going to be placed in the range of 3250. Also, we have used the data-scale value of 3.5 which allows us to show six portfolio items in the overview. Depending on the number of items you have to increase or decrease the scale value.

Apart from impress attributes, we have used a custom attribute called data-type and it's going to be used for handling step transitions in later stages. Let's take a look at the portfolio gallery with six items:

Portfolio single

This page will contain the complete details about a single item. The following is a screenshot of the portfolio single page:

If we compare the previous screen of the overview and the single item screen, we can definitely see that the same step has different content. Let's first look at the implementation of portfolio items to understand the difference:

```
<div id="portfolio-1" class="step slide portfolio" data-x="1900"
    data-y='0' data-type="portfolio" >
    <div class="large"><img src="images/portfolio-large.png" /></div>
    <div class="small">
        // Details with small image
    </div>
</div>

<div id="portfolio-2" class="step slide portfolio" data-x="3200"
    data-y='0' data-type="portfolio" >
    <div class="large"><img src="images/portfolio-large.png" /></div>
    <div class="small">
        // Details with small image
    </div>
</div>
```

After the overview step, we place the portfolio items one by one. A special class called `portfolio` is used to provide portfolio-specific design. Each item contains a container with the class `small` and `large`. These will be used as two separate sections. At any given time, one of these containers will be made visible.

We use the container with the class `large` for the overview page and it will be visible by default. The container with class `small` is used for the detailed page and it's kept invisible initially. Once the step transition happens from overview to single item, the visibility of these containers needs to be switched.

Let's see how to handle step transitions using impress events:

```
document.addEventListener("impress:stepenter", function (event) {
    var data_type = $(".active").attr("data-type");
    if(data_type == 'portfolio'){
        $(".active .small").show();
        $(".active .large").hide();
    }else if(data_type == 'portfolio-gallery'){
        $(".small").hide();
        $(".large").show();
    }
}, false);
```

First we assign the stepenter event of impress.js into the current document. Both the portfolio overview and single step has an attribute called data-type. The data type of the active step is assigned to a variable and will be conditionally checked for different steps.

When the portfolio gallery becomes active, we hide the detailed view and display the large image preview. Similarly, when the portfolio item becomes active, we hide the large container and display the details with the small container.

Currently, the stepenter event has two conditional checks. We will be adding more conditions as we move further into creating the other pages.

> In the overview, a large image is displayed. Since there are three images inside the screen you will think that the size of the image is very small. Don't be misled as the overview is a scaled version. The actual image size will be the same as the size of the presentation step container.

Now we have completed the home page and portfolio pages of the website.

Designing the timeline page

Timelines are very popular components among websites. They allow us to track the time of various activities. We are going to create a different kind of timeline with impress.js effects to show the important activities of your career. Working knowledge of 3D space is required to create the timeline. We will be using the depth of the presentation canvas using the data-z attribute. Let's take a look at the preview of our timeline:

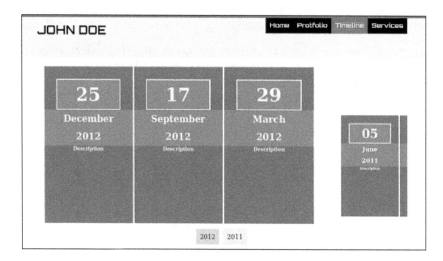

You can see that all the events of 2012 are displayed with the same size, and the events of 2011 seem to be smaller compared to the 2012 events. Actually, the 2011 events are created with the same dimensions as the 2012 events, but they are placed deeper in the presentation canvas using the data-z attribute.

So, the events of the current year are displayed initially. Past years are placed deeper and deeper into the canvas. This effect enables us to view the latest event closest to us and go into the screen for the previous events. Hence the effect we used adds meaning to the timeline. Now let's see the implementation:

```
<div id="timeline-step1" class="step slide timeline" data-x="6300"
data-y='0' data-year="2012" data-type="timeline">
  //content
</div>
<div id="timeline-step2" class="step slide timeline" data-x="6600"
data-y='0' data-year="2012" data-type="timeline" >
  //content
</div>
<div id="timeline-step3" class="step slide timeline str-2011"
data-x="7200" data-y='100' data-z="-700" data-year="2011" data-
type="timeline" >
  //content
</div>
```

Here, I have given three steps from the timeline. The inner content is omitted here for explanatory purposes. You can see that the two steps of 2012 have the same data-y values and varying data-x values. The data-z value is not specified, which means it is the same for both of the steps. Then, you can see that the step of 2011 is placed with the data-z value of -700 which means it's deeper in the screen than 2012. In case you are defining steps for 2010, you should use the data-z value of something like -1400. Now let's see how events for 2011 are displayed:

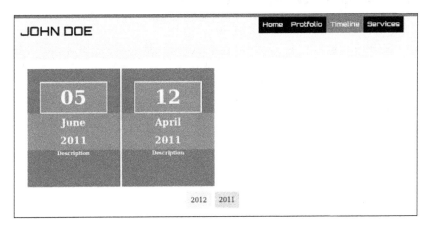

Since there are no events for 2010, nothing will be displayed on the right of the 2011 steps. At the bottom, we are showing the years available in the timeline and the year of the current step. Let's see how we can implement this feature.

Defining the timeline navigation

Once the presentation is completely loaded we can use the `data-year` attribute of the timeline steps to generate the navigation bar with available years.

```
$(document).ready(function(){
    var timeline_years=[];
    $(".timeline").each(function(){
        var year = $(this).attr("data-year");
        if(($.inArray(year, timeline_years)) == -1){
            timeline_years.push(year);
            $("#timeline_tracker").append("<span id='nav-"+year+"'
            data-year='"+year+"'>"+year+"</span>");
        }
    });
});
```

Once the document is ready, we get the distinct years by traversing through the `data-year` attribute of timeline steps and push it to an array. We use an `inArray` function to identify the distinct years. Then, we add each year as control buttons to the `timeline_tracker` container using jQuery's `append` function.

Initially, the `timeline_tracker` container is defined in the page with the `display:none` attribute. Let's now see how we can make it visible on step transfer:

```
document.addEventListener("impress:stepenter", function (event) {
    $("#timeline_tracker").hide();
    $("#timeline_tracker span").removeClass("year-highlight");

    var data_type = $(".active").attr("data-type");
    if(data_type == 'timeline'){
        $("#timeline_tracker").show();
        var data_year = $(".active").attr("data-year");
        $("#nav-"+data_year).addClass("year-highlight");
    }

}, false);
```

Earlier, we created the `stepenter` event for portfolio item management. This code will be added to the same function with another `else if` statement. Initially, we hide the `timeline_tracker` container and remove the highlighting class on each step transfer. Then, we check whether the active step is part of the timeline. In such cases, we make the `timeline_tracker` container visible and assign the highlight class to the year of the currently active step.

Now we have navigations and highlighting for years in the timeline. Before we complete this, we have to make sure to create the navigation functionality for the year buttons, as shown in the following code:

```
$("body").on("click", "#timeline_tracker span", function(){
    var year = $(this).attr("data-year");
    var start_step = $(".str-"+year).attr("id");
    api.goto(start_step);
});
```

jQuery's on function can be used to add events to dynamically inserted DOM elements. We assign an anonymous function to the click events of timeline years. Once the year is clicked, we get the value using the `data-year` attribute. Then, we use the `goto` function of impress.js to navigate to the selected step.

Designing the services page

Throughout the previous sections, we used impress effects such as transform and scaling to provide functionality for pages. Now, we are going to develop our last page of the website by using rotation effects. First, we have to create the main page of our services section. This will be a basic step and hence no code explanation will be needed. The following is a preview of our services home page:

We are going to use rotations around the x axis for the individual service pages. Let's move into the implementation right away:

```
<div id="services-step1" class="step slide services" data-x="-1400"
data-y="-300" data-rotate-x="0" >
    <div class="service-desc">WordPress Plugin Develoment</div>
</div>
<div id="services-step2" class="step slide services" data-x="-1400"
data-z="-300" data-y="0"  data-rotate-x="90" >
    <div class="service-desc">WordPress Theme Design</div>
</div>
<div id="services-step3" class="step slide services" data-x="-1400"
data-y="400"   data-rotate-x="180" >
    <div class="service-desc">Freelance Article Writing</div>
</div>
<div id="services-step4" class="step slide services" data-x="-1400"
data-z="300" data-y="100"  data-rotate-x="270" >
    <div class="service-desc">PHP Development</div>
</div>
```

The important thing here is the placements of steps. Locating steps with rotations is the most difficult part in building presentations with impress.js. We have thus kept the data-x value of all the four steps to the same value.

Then, each of the steps is rotated at a 90 degree angle across the x axis using the data-rotate-x attribute. Two of the slides will be in one direction while the other two will be in the opposite direction with a 180 degree angle. We have to use the data-y attribute for steps in the same direction and the data-z attribute for the other two steps in the same direction. The value of the attribute depends on how you want to place these steps. Try changing the values until you get the correct positioning. Once the service detail pages are implemented, it should look similar to the following screenshot:

Handling the navigation menu

At the start of this chapter, we looked at the header with the navigation menu. Now let's implement the navigation links and controls. We have to assign unique IDs to the steps that we want appearing on the menu. Here I have assigned the IDs of the four pages for the href attribute of the menu:

```
<ul>
    <li id="menu-about" ><a href="#/about">Home</a></li>
    <li id="menu-portfolio-overview" ><a href=
    "#/portfolio-overview">Protfolio</a></li>
    <li id="menu-timeline-start" ><a href=
    "#/timeline-start">Timeline</a></li>
    <li id="menu-services-overview" ><a href=
    "#/services-overview">Services</a></li>
</ul>
```

Whenever the user clicks on the link, the presentation will navigate to the step with the specified ID. Also, you may have noticed that we have used the same ID for the list item with menu- as the prefix. We are going to use this ID to highlight the active menu. Let's get on with the implementation for highlighting:

```
document.addEventListener("impress:stepenter", function (event) {
    var data_id = $(".active").attr("id");
    if(data_id == 'about'){
        $("li").removeClass("menu_highlight");
        $("#menu-about").addClass("menu_highlight");
    }else if(data_id == 'portfolio-overview'){
        $("li").removeClass("menu_highlight");
        $("#menu-portfolio-overview").addClass("menu_highlight");
    }else if(data_id == 'timeline-start'){
        $("li").removeClass("menu_highlight");
        $("#menu-timeline-start").addClass("menu_highlight");
    }else if(data_id == 'services-overview'){
        $("li").removeClass("menu_highlight");
        $("#menu-services-overview").addClass("menu_highlight");
    }
}, false);
```

On the stepenter event we get the ID of the active step. Then, we check if it's one of the main menu items. If a match is found we remove the menu highlighting class from all other menu items and assign it to the currently active menu. So, whenever we move between steps, the main menu item will be displayed in a different color.

Creating the navigation hint

Since we are creating a website using impress.js, users have the ability to use keyboard navigations to traverse through various pages. But the users don't know that this website is built upon impress.js. This means we have to provide a hint indicating to users to use keyboard controls. A hint is created as a separate component from the presentation as shown in the following code:

```
<div class="hint">
    <p>Use a spacebar or arrow keys to navigate</p>
</div>
```

This container should be placed after the wrapper container. Now, we don't need to show the hint in every step, so we are going to limit the hint to the home page. Initially the hint will be kept hidden with opacity of 0. When the impress presentation is initialized, we set display to block using the following CSS code:

```
.impress-enabled .hint {
    display: block;
}
```

Since opacity is set to 0, it is not displayed yet to the user. So, let's enable the hint on the home page using the following code snippet:

```
.impress-on-about .hint {
    opacity: 1;
    transform: translateY(0px);
    transition: opacity 1s ease 1s, transform 0.5s ease 1s;
}
```

Impress generates a class called impress-on-{stepId} in each step transition. The home page will thus contain a class called impress-on-about when active. We set the opacity to 1 to make it visible to the user.

Now, we have designed and developed a fully functional personal website using impress.js. You can change the details to your own information and host it online to get a better online reputation.

Summary

In the previous chapters we learned how impress.js can be used to create presentations. In this chapter, we focused on creating something different from its default behavior.

We chose to create a personal website with impress.js as having a personal website can be an effective way of increasing your reputation online. We started by designing a complete website from scratch. Throughout this chapter, we assigned impress effects to real-world scenarios and created four different types of pages for the site.

By now you should be familiar with all kinds of possibilities of working with impress.js. In the next chapter, we are going to discuss the issues and bugs of impress.js and how we can effectively manage them without distracting the users.

Until then, make sure you try creating your own website and host it online.

6
Troubleshooting

No technologies or libraries are without bugs and issues at the beginning of their development. impress.js also has its share of bugs and limitations. As developers or designers, we should be capable of handling bugs and creating workarounds.

impress.js has an active community and hence you can report bugs or limitations and get solutions very quickly. This chapter will focus on providing the necessary knowledge to troubleshoot impress.js presentations when required.

In this chapter, we are going to cover the following topics:

- Browser compatibility
- Handling unsupported browsers
- Limitations and new features
- Troubleshooting and support

Browser compatibility

Even though impress.js is a presentation framework, it runs inside the browser window, so the compatibility of browsers needs to be taken into consideration when creating presentations. Let's take a look at supported and unsupported browsers and devices for impress.js.

impress.js uses transforms of CSS3 and hence it is mainly supported in web browsers, compared to mobile browsers. The following is the list of supported browsers for impress.js:

- Firefox Version 10 and higher
- Safari Version 5.1 and higher
- Chrome
- Internet Explorer 10 (needs additional polyfill libraries)

Currently, impress.js provides very limited support for mobile-based devices. The following is the list of supported devices for impress.js:

- iPad
- BlackBerry PlayBook

If you are using impress.js for presenting information, make sure you use one of the three browsers which provide comprehensive support. In case you are creating websites or applications accessed by online users, it's preferable to mention the supported browsers.

The following is a list of unsupported browsers for impress.js:

- Opera
- Internet Explorer 9 and lower
- Mobile browsers

Also, it's mentioned on the official site that you need to have hardware acceleration support to run the impress animations smoothly. Even though they don't work on some browsers, there is a good chance that those browsers will provide support for CSS 3D transforms in the near future.

Handling unsupported browsers

In browsers which do not have the support for impress.js, presentation steps will be displayed all over the place without proper alignment or design which can make it very hard to read. Since users don't have a clear idea about impress.js, it's common that they will consider it as a bad design which is going to ruin your reputation as a designer.

It is thus recommended to provide a notification for users using unsupported browsers. impress.js has an in-built method to provide this functionality using CSS classes. There are two predefined classes called `impress-supported` and `impress-not-supported`. When the browser is not supported, the `impress-not-supported` class will be assigned to the body element and when the browser is fully compatible, the `impress-supported` class is added to the body.

Now let's create the fallback message for the user. The following is the message used in the default official demo:

```
<div class="fallback-message">
    <p>Your browser <b>doesn't support the features required</b> by
impress.js, so you are presented with a simplified version of this
presentation.</p>
    <p>For the best experience please use the latest <b>Chrome</b>,
<b>Safari</b> or <b>Firefox</b> browser.</p>
</div>
```

We can place this element anywhere in the page inside the body tag and change the messages when necessary. There are two ways of displaying this message to the user. First, we can hide the fallback message and display on unsupported browsers using following CSS code:

```
.impress-not-supported .fallback-message {
    display: block;
}
```

The second method is to display the fallback message initially and hide them in the supported browsers using following CSS code:

```
.impress-supported .fallback-message {
    display: none;
}
```

Limitations and new features

impress.js was built to create presentations even though we are interested in some amazing other applications with the framework. It is improving every day and there are a few limitations in some scenarios. Also, there are new functionalities which might add a tremendous boost to the power of impress presentations. In this section, we are going to figure out the limitations and necessary improvements that we are hoping to see in the future. We will look into the following list in this section:

- Positioning steps relative to other steps
- Defining the previous and next steps

- Transition duration for individual steps
- Adding and removing navigation keys
- Creating substeps

Positioning steps relative to other steps

We define the positioning of elements using the `data-x`, `data-y`, and `data-z` attributes. For each step, we need to provide absolute values such as `data-x=100` and `data-x=300` , but it would be more appropriate to position steps relative to each other using syntax similar to the following:

```
<div class="step" data-x="100">
  <div>Step1</div>
</div>
<div class="step" data-x+="300">
  <div>Step1</div>
</div>
```

In this scenario, the second step will be 300px to the right-hand side of the first step. Providing relative positions allows us to have a clear understanding about the margins between steps rather than calculating it.

Defining the previous and next steps

Presentations are not always going to be run step by step in a sequential manner. Sometimes we need to go to the previously explained slide and then move to the next slide without proper ordering. With current impress functions, it's a little difficult. In the slider automation example, we created a workaround to go to any step we like. But it is some additional work. It would be more appropriate if impress. js could provide something like the following:

```
<div id="step1" class="step" data-x="100">
  <div>Step1</div>
</div>
<div id="step2" class="step" data-x="300" data-previous="step1" data-next="step3" >
  <div>Step2</div>
</div>
<div id="step3" class="step" data-x="300" data-previous="step1" data-next="step2">
  <div>Step3</div>
</div>
```

In this situation, we will be able to define the next and previous steps of any given slide using a simple data attribute inside the step. This will be a very handy feature which we can expect to see in the future.

Transition duration for individual steps

We can provide transition durations for slides in the impress container using the `data-transition-duration` attribute with existing functionality, but the timing will be the same for all the steps. Defining durations for each step can be a very useful feature. We can use syntax like the following to define the transition duration for individual items:

```
<div class="step" data-x="300" data-duration="3000" >
  <div>Step2</div>
</div>
<div class="step" data-x="300" data-duration="2000" >
  <div>Step2</div>
</div>
```

Adding and removing navigation keys

Adding or removing a key used for navigation is very difficult without changing the core impress.js library. It is not wise to change the library for such a task as it reduces the extendibility of the library. Since it is common throughout the presentation, we cannot define data attributes as we did earlier, so we have to write some kind of API method to add and remove keys when necessary, and add custom functionality for new keys.

Creating substeps

We are allowed to create as many steps as we want. Sometimes we need small substeps to be shown inside the main steps. There is no way to provide such functionality with the current version of impress.js. We thus have to implement this feature in the future.

The limitations we mentioned can be converted to add real power to impress presentations. impress.js is open source and free. So why don't you try to implement these features in your own impress version?

Troubleshooting and support

impress.js is not only used for presentations. We might find bugs on the core framework when we are trying to provide custom functionalities for our applications. It's our responsibility to report such bugs using the official Github site. impress.js has an active support forum where people will solve the bugs or new features in core impress.js or their own branched versions of impress.js. Once we identify an issue, first we have to go through the existing and fixed bugs list to see whether it has already been taken into consideration. Otherwise, you will have to report it and look for answers from the people who are using and developing impress.js.

The following screenshot shows us a list of existing and fixed bugs:

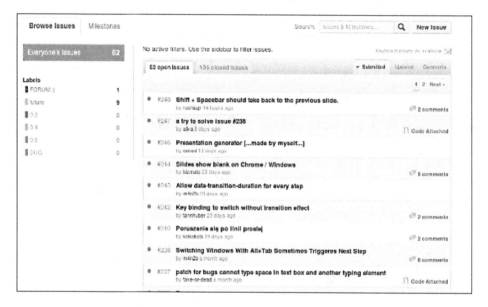

All your new ideas and feature requests should be submitted using the http://github.com/bartaz/impress.js/issues/new link. The active issues list can be found at https://github.com/bartaz/impress.js/issues.

Summary

Throughout this book we learned about various types of presentations and techniques using impress.js. Since every library has its limitations and issues, we need to have the proper knowledge to fix those issues without much trouble.

We identified the limitations and issues of impress.js and discussed possible solutions to get around them. Finally we learnt where to look for support in case we are not capable of fixing errors, so we discussed how to report bugs and get your issues resolved using the Github site for impress.js.

Now we have come to the end of creating impressive presentations with impress.js. You should be capable of building different kinds of presentations with impress. In *Appendix, Impress Tools and Resources*, we will be looking at some of the cool impress presentations and applications.

Impress Tools and Resources

We covered the impress.js presentation development techniques and concepts in the previous chapters. Once you are familiar with creating presentations, there are some online resources to improve your experience on this framework. Covering these tools and applications is beyond the scope of this book, so you can go through these resources online.

Impress presentation tools

In order to create impress presentations, you must at least have knowledge of HTML and CSS. Not everyone who wants to create presentations will be familiar with these technologies, so it's important to find out the possibilities of creating impress presentations without technical knowledge. Luckily, there are some free tools we can use to create presentations with impress.js.

Strut

This is a free tool where you can create slides with basic elements. Although it is not possible to use the full features of impress.js, this will be handy for non-technical people to create quick presentations. You can find this tool available at `http://tantaman.github.com/Strut/dist/index.html`.

As with most presentation software, slides are displayed as a list in the left-hand side and we can add new slides dynamically. The following screenshot will preview the slide creation screen of this tool:

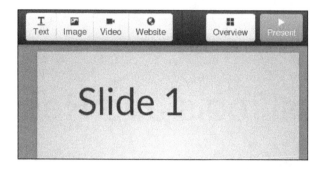

We can add elements such as text, images, and videos into slides. Advanced features such as CSS styles and events cannot be used yet with this tool. Once we finish the slide creation process, we can go to the overview of the presentation using the **Overview** button on the right. The **Overview** screen will be as follows:

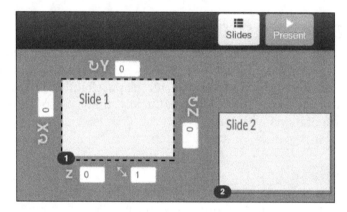

Overview is where we position our slides. Just drag the slides or provide custom values for the x, y, z attributes. Once we are done with adjusting the positions, we can click on the **Present** button to start the presentation and it will run as a normal impress presentation.

Impressionist

Impressionist is another tool to automate the presentation creation process. You can find the demo at `http://hsivaram.com/impressionist/0.1/`. The only limitation of impressionist compared to strut is that it only works on WebKit browsers, so we will be using the Chrome browser to demonstrate the functionality.

The following is the main slide creation screen of impressionist. It is quite similar to the previous slide creation screen:

Once we are done with all the slides, we can move into the overview of slides using the **Orchestration View** button on the top-right corner of the screen. There you can position elements like we did earlier. All the controls are given in the menu bar for positioning, rotating, and scaling. The following is the preview of **Orchestration View**:

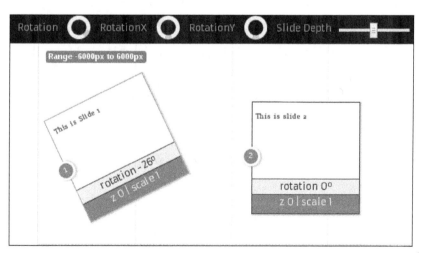

We can click on the **Preview** button to see the presentation in action. These tools are very handy for non-technical users. Feel free to check out these tools and create simplified presentations.

Impressive presentations

We have created various kinds of presentations throughout this book. Now let's see some awesome presentations created by others using impress.js:

- What the Heck is Responsive Web Design by John Polacek at `http://johnpolacek.github.com/WhatTheHeckIsResponsiveWebDesign-impressjs/#/title`

- `12412.org` presentation to Digibury by Stephen Fulljames at `http://extra.12412.org/digibury/#/title`

- Bonne année 2012 by Edouard Cunibil at `http://duael.fr/voeux/2012/#/since-2009`

- WordPress 201: Performance and Security by Jason Cosper at `http://jasoncosper.com/talks/wcphx/wp201/#/step-1`

- The Revolutionary CSS3: a non-technical intro to CSS3 by Scott Cheng at `http://scottcheng.github.com/revolutionary-css3/#/title`

impress.js demos from the book

We created sample applications to explain each concept and technique in impress.js in this book. Here you can find the online resources for accessing these demos.

A complete list of all the demos from the book can be found at the following link:

`http://innovativephp.com/demo/impress-js-demos/`

Full source code of the examples in this book can be downloaded from the following link:

`http://innovativephp.com/demo/impress-js-demos.zip`

Index

S

scaling
  combining, with positioning 34
  data perspective 37-39
  practical application, creating 35, 36
scaling effects 32, 33
scrollTo function 50
services page
  designing 87, 88
setInterval function 51, 64, 66
setTimeout function 53
slide creation screen, Impressionist 103
slide creation screen, Strut 102
slides
  about 8
  designing 63, 64
step class 15
  working 55
step click event
  handling 59, 60
stepenter event 53-89
stepleave event 53, 54, 67
steps
  about 8
  creating 14, 15, 16
  defining 96
  positioning, relative to other steps 96
  styles, applying 15, 16
  visibility, limiting 18
step_transitions array 52
Strut
  about 101
  slide creation screen 102
  URL 101
styles
  applying, on steps 15, 16
substeps
  creating 97
switch statement 58, 59

T

themes, impress.js 11
timeline navigation
  defining 86, 87
timeline page
  designing, for website 84, 85

timelines 84
timeline_tracker container 87
transition-duration attribute 97
translate3d function 41

U

unsupported browsers
  handling 94, 95

V

visibility
  limiting, of steps 18
visibility attribute 18

W

web-based presentations 7
website structure
  header, designing 76
  planning 76
  presentation wrapper, designing 77, 78

X

x axis
  effects, positioning on 23
  elements, rotating around 26, 27

Y

y axis
  effects, positioning on 24
  elements, rotating around 27, 28

Z

z axis
  effects, positioning on 24, 25
  elements, rotating around 28
zoom-in feature 15
zoom-out feature 15

Thank you for buying
Building Impressive Presentations with impress.js

About Packt Publishing

Packt, pronounced 'packed', published its first book "*Mastering phpMyAdmin for Effective MySQL Management*" in April 2004 and subsequently continued to specialize in publishing highly focused books on specific technologies and solutions.

Our books and publications share the experiences of your fellow IT professionals in adapting and customizing today's systems, applications, and frameworks. Our solution based books give you the knowledge and power to customize the software and technologies you're using to get the job done. Packt books are more specific and less general than the IT books you have seen in the past. Our unique business model allows us to bring you more focused information, giving you more of what you need to know, and less of what you don't.

Packt is a modern, yet unique publishing company, which focuses on producing quality, cutting-edge books for communities of developers, administrators, and newbies alike. For more information, please visit our website: www.packtpub.com.

About Packt Open Source

In 2010, Packt launched two new brands, Packt Open Source and Packt Enterprise, in order to continue its focus on specialization. This book is part of the Packt Open Source brand, home to books published on software built around Open Source licences, and offering information to anybody from advanced developers to budding web designers. The Open Source brand also runs Packt's Open Source Royalty Scheme, by which Packt gives a royalty to each Open Source project about whose software a book is sold.

Writing for Packt

We welcome all inquiries from people who are interested in authoring. Book proposals should be sent to author@packtpub.com. If your book idea is still at an early stage and you would like to discuss it first before writing a formal book proposal, contact us; one of our commissioning editors will get in touch with you.

We're not just looking for published authors; if you have strong technical skills but no writing experience, our experienced editors can help you develop a writing career, or simply get some additional reward for your expertise.

Mastering Prezi for Business Presentations

ISBN: 978-1-849693-02-8   Paperback: 258 pages

Engage your audience visually with stunning Prezi presentation designs and be the envy of your colleagues who use PowerPoint

1. Turns anyone already using Prezi into a master of both design and delivery

2. Illustrated throughout with easy to follow screenshots and some live Prezi examples to view online

3. Written by Russell Anderson-Williams, one of the fourteen experts hand-picked by Prezi

Responsive Web Design with HTML5 and CSS3

ISBN: 978-1-849693-18-9   Paperback: 324 pages

Learn responsive design using HTML5 and CSS3 to adapt websites to any browser or screen size

1. Everything needed to code websites in HTML5 and CSS3 that are responsive to every device or screen size

2. Learn the main new features of HTML5 and use CSS3's stunning new capabilities including animations, transitions, and transformations

3. Real world examples show how to progressively enhance a responsive design while providing fall backs for older browsers

Please check **www.PacktPub.com** for information on our titles

WebGL Beginner's Guide

ISBN: 978-1-849691-72-7   Paperback: 376 pages

Become a master of 3D web programming in WebGL and JavaScript

1. Dive headfirst into 3D web application development using WebGL and JavaScript.

2. Each chapter is loaded with code examples and exercises that allow the reader to quickly learn the various concepts associated with 3D web development

3. The only software that the reader needs to run the examples is an HTML5 enabled modern web browser. No additional tools needed.

HTML5 Canvas Cookbook

ISBN: 978-1-849691-36-9   Paperback: 348 pages

Over 80 recepies to revolutionalize the web experience with HTML5 Canvas

1. The quickest way to get up to speed with HTML5 Canvas application and game development

2. Create stunning 3D visualizations and games without Flash

4. Written in a modern, unobtrusive, and objected oriented JavaScript style so that the code can be reused in your own applications.

Please check **www.PacktPub.com** for information on our titles

www.ingramcontent.com/pod-product-compliance
Lightning Source LLC
LaVergne TN
LVHW080100070326
832902LV00014B/2333